FROM THE PLAIN OF THE YEW TREE

THE LIFETIME JOURNEY

OF A

COUNTY MAYO MUSICIAN

by

John Hoban

Edited by Kate Donnelly

ORIGINAL WRITING

ISBN: 978-1-907179-87-7

A cip catalogue for this book is available from the National Library.

Published by Original Writing Ltd., Dublin, 2010.

Printed by Cahill Printers Limited, Dublin.

Oct. 26th
2010.

This book is dedicated to the music in us all,
an ceol ó dhúcas ionainn go léir.

with
every best
wish to you
from John Hoban

A Note on the Photographs

The front and back cover photographs were taken in a café in Dublin and south of Beltra, County Mayo by Steven Weekes.

Isabela and I took all the other photographs in the book during our travels together, with the exception of the photograph of me, taken by John Galayda (Chapter 8).

A guide to the photographs at the beginning of each chapter:

Chapter 1, Swans in Loch Lannagh, Castlebar, County Mayo, Ireland.

Chapter 2, Downpatrick Head, County Mayo, Ireland.

Chapter 3, The Jaguar Stone, Peruvian Andes.

Chapter 4, Nephin Mountain, Windy Gap, County Mayo, Ireland.

Chapter 5, The Sacred Valley, Peruvian Andes.

Chapter 6, Clare Island, County Mayo, Ireland.

Chapter 7, Na Bri, Brieze, County Mayo, Ireland.

Chapter 8, John Hoban.

Chapter 9, Travelling by plane, South America.

Chapter 10, 'On the road', Orange County, California, USA.

Chapter 11, Machu Picchu, Peru.

Epilogue, The Peruvian Andes.

Acknowledgements

I would like to thank my editor and friend Kate Donnelly for her wonderful work. Her technical abilities coupled with great discernment made her contribution invaluable. I would also like to thank Geraldine Mitchell for her professional support to Kate in the editing process.

Míle buíchas to Éadaoin Donnelly-White and Leo Green for their powerful work on the Irish language throughout the book. Gach bua agus beannacht.

My thanks also go to:

Mattie Lennon for pointing me towards the publishers, Original Writing Limited.

Garrett Bonner and Steven Weekes from Original Writing for their top-class work.

Christy Moore for his friendship, fellowship and music.

To The Shamrogues and the Wild Geese for their support over the years and over the Atlantic.

The many musicians who encouraged and heartened me, too many to mention here.

My own family and Isabela's family for their kindness and support.

And finally, a big thank you to my wife, Isabela, who helped and inspired me from day one.

A Note from the Author

A new book, *From the Plain of the Yew Tree* has just been born. Plain of the yew tree is the literal English translation of Mayo (Muigh Eo, or Maigh Eo). While the writing of this book is a fairly recent event, the life within it has been lived, sung and walked for just over half a century. Fifty-six years to be precise. The book came together just as a song does, first an idea, then a tune, finally taking off on a life of its own – revisiting my life in music. I wrote this book to mark my own individual path of learning and playing music, and to document a time of change in musical culture and life during my own lifetime.

The story is all about music. Not exactly how music is presented today by the mass media where music has become a commodity that must sell. It seems as if its very right to exist depends on popularity and commercial value. The story in these pages is about one person's first and final language. All through my life, music has served, and continues to serve, as a soul friend to me, a guide, a teacher, a prophet, a warrior and a means to survival in the world. Music, for me, has always been the sound of truth, the sound of love, the sound of hate and the sound of where we all are situated in creation. The story describes an individual, creative and original way to live in music through the various struggles we all encounter on life's pathway.

I have written my story as a mixture of life memories, songs and poems. We travel from my birth in Maigh Eo, and follow my growing up there in the '50s and '60s. My meandering path takes us then to Dublin, London, back to Ireland in search of music and meaning, on 'out foreign' and finally, back to earth again.

My writing explores in depth many aspects of music. For example, I talk about how I learned to play many different musical instruments in various styles without having received any formal tuition. I talk about how I perceive music education and how music should be 'passed on'. This book also looks at how music affects every aspect of our lives and reaches all communities, the elderly, those suffering with addictions and people from different cultures. The story covers street music, music composition and performance. These recollections are written from my own experiences. I have learned everything I know from being 'on the road'.

I want my story to be a true sharing of insights into the real, inner world of songs and dance, airs and graces.

This story also honours the gift of music. It pays homage to those who took the time to pass the music on with much wisdom and great kindness. I continue trying my best each day to live my life well, and to carry the message of an honest, joyful life in ceol/music to my fellow brothers and sisters.

John C. Hoban.

John Hoban
14th July 2010
Castlebar

Foreword

Johnny's new book is called *From the Plain of the Yew Tree*. That's where we always meet.

I was walkin' down The Rocks in Sydney, feeling lonesome and jet lagged. There was a familiar thirst rising within me when I got a tap on the shoulder – it was Johnny Hoban, sent to me by my Guardian Angel. He took me to a tea-room, spoke quietly to me, and before I knew it, we were locked into the 'White Space'. We flew to Castlebar and heard Raymond Roland on the way. In with us to The Cobblestone where Johnny Mulhearn was singing 'Delaney's Gone Back on the Wine'. Over to the Five Lamps for a hit of Wally Page, and then we took a walk by the Sydney Opera House and talked to the Thirsty Ducks. "There, but for the grace of God..." says Johnny.

He sorted me out with his healing caint (talk). Meeting Johnny Hoban is always like a good fleadh cheoil for me. I look forward to lingering with him upon 'the plain of the yew tree'. He is a pillar in my life. Nelson would only be in the ha'penny place. Take me home to Mayo Johnny Hoban...

Christy Moore
3rd July 2010

Contents

FROM THE PLAIN OF THE YEW TREE

THE LIFETIME JOURNEY
OF A
COUNTY MAYO MUSICIAN

Chapter 1

Tús Maith Leath na hOibre
A Good Start is Half the Work

Tell me what I need to know,
I'm willing to change, I'm letting go.
I want to be like a stream
down a mountainside...
('On my Side', John Hoban)

Music, songs, stories and listening have given me life
and hope from birth to this day. They have mapped
out the road, four directions along a strange, confus-
ing, beautiful path. Music always made me feel that all would
be well someday, that it would all work out for the better. Here's
the full story.

I believe I was born on St. Brigid's Eve, 31st January, 1954, in
County Mayo, 'the plain of the yew tree'. The twelve o'clock An-
gelus bells where ringing out over the town of Castlebar. My earliest memories are, needless to say, very sketchy, but I do know
that both my parents were deeply connected to music. My father,
Christy, was a singer of songs, both ballads and light opera. He
sang 'The Maid of Sweet Brown Knowe' and also starred, big
time, in *Lilac Time* by Schubert and Gilbert and Sullivan's *The
Mikado*. In those times, both Castlebar and Westport (my father's
home town) would have had very good church choirs and 'musical
societies', as they were known. As a child I remember hearing the
local postman humming arias from *La Bohème*, a house painter
whistling tunes from *Madame Butterfly*, while carpenters and
other tradesmen would be singing 'Boulavogue' and 'The Croppy
Boy'. The Latin Mass also featured in my everyday life – talk about
an eclectic mix. My father was part of that musical setup.

1

My mother, Nancy Byrne, came from Newantrim Street, Castlebar. Herself and her sisters were very highly regarded dancers in the Irish tradition. At one stage, I heard, they used to give lessons in Glenhest Hall. Her only brother was a County Mayo footballer, Tommy was his name. The Byrnes hailed from East Mayo, a place called Cloonterrif near the town of Knock. Many years after my mother passed away, I went back to visit my relatives, and I felt like the prodigal son of old. I was so happy to be back there, and I was happier still to learn about the wealth of music on that side of my family. I knew very little about my mother's family as she passed away in 1967 when I was thirteen years of age.

So, as they say, *the apple doesn't fall far from the tree*, or, as the Irish proverb says, *Is dual dó bheith ceolmhar* (it's his nature to be musical). This book is an exploration and an explanation of my own relationship with music. The year of 1954 was a highly significant year in the history of modern music. The great Elvis Presley was giving his heart and soul in Sun Studios, Memphis, Tennessee at the time. They called it rock'n'roll and rockabilly. A sister of my father's, Patricia, or Auntie Pat, worked as a nurse all her life. For a large slice of years she lived and worked in a hospital in New York City. I was delighted when she informed me that, as a baby, I used to wake up singing. She couldn't remember the songs I was giving but maybe it was 'That's Alright Mama' or 'John O'Dreams'. Imagine waking up singing.

The songs I heard in my infancy and childhood were hugely important to me. They informed me about both inner and outer realities – or worlds – of which I was becoming aware. I think of music as survival, life and death, a sort of scout, a guide, the truth, the dream catcher, the shield, the road to enlightenment and many more things.

One of my earliest memories as a very small child is feeling that I was actually *physically* connected to Dubh Loch (black lake) and Mweelrea Mountain. I remember feeling like I wanted to be the stream flowing down the mountain into the lake, and then on out to the ocean. I experienced the same feeling years later and wrote it into the song 'On My Side' (quoted at the beginning of this chapter).

All the major times and changes in my life are marked by music. All the future is pointed out by music; sometimes it comes to me in dreams. Music is the locus of my existence.

Hush little baby,
don't you cry.
You know your daddy
was born to die.
All my trials Lord,
will soon be over.
('All my Trials', Traditional)

The above song was on an old vanguard LP by Joan Baez. She also sang 'Mary Hamilton' and 'Kum Ba Yah' on the same recording. I still sing these songs. When I sing them, I am transported back to my earliest musical/life memories on Westport Road, Castlebar.

We had a really lovely back garden outside our house. It was big enough to stage a game of football, but too narrow for a game of hurling or a rock concert. As a small child, I recall a great variety of birds visiting every day. They sang a lot, and they also scrapped for the food which we gave to them. I often sat in the shade of a lilac bush, in a cot, listening to them sing their inspiring songs.

My first memory of live music, traditional Irish music, was when we visited relatives of my father's in Leitir Broc, behind Croagh Patrick mountain. On a couple of other occasions, when I was a baby, we visited my mother's relatives in Cloonterrif . These visits meant the world to me. I am not sure how the other people felt about this music, but *my* earliest memories are crystal clear. The music these people were playing felt like everything to me. It felt like life or death, sheer wonder, safety and comfort. Years later, these music-filled visits came back to help me through life's trials.

3

So, my father's singing, my mother's singing and dancing, Uncle Dom's fiddle music and the Byrnes, my brother and sisters' singing, the music from the Sheaffry Hills and Carrowkennedy, the church choir, the Latin Mass, Stephen Garvey, the wireless, mother nature, the sounds from the Royal Ballroom of a Sunday night, all contributed greatly to a very rich world of music, song and dance. However, I became aware of two worlds happening at once, the inner and the outer. The inner spiritual world was real and infinite and natural to me. The outer world was a show. A showdown perhaps, a maze of little paths going in all directions. I didn't trust it. I listened and tried to meditate so I might hear the true sound of the soul. The truth, in other words. Music did set me free but first I had to live it. I had to believe in it. I had to believe so that I could see. I had to feel the pain and the freedom of being a musicianer from day one.

There is a house in New Orleans
they call the Risin' Sun.
It's been the ruin
of many's a poor boy.
God, I know I'm one.
('House of the Rising Sun', Traditional)

This was the first song I learned to sing with the guitar and harmonica. I figured it out myself, and thankfully I am free, for today, from the ball and chain of slavery referred to in this great song.

I have spent my whole life living in music, walking my own songline into creation.

CASTLE LANE

(John Hoban)

Castle Lane, Castlebar 1954,
the bacon house of high renown,
Christy at the door.
The nuns looked down on our backyard,
the convent was a castle.
My father met my mother there,
many years ago. Many days ago.

Christy was a bacon-hand,
he was 15-carat 'Covey'.
Served his time in Glasgow,
his people came from Sheaffry.
He always wore a clean, white coat.
Drove a Vauxhall car.
Served the great and not so great,
in the town of Castlebar,
in the town of Castlebar.

The street had every kind of shop selling
porter, nails and hatpins. A watchmaker, a
shoemaker, a special house for ice-cream,
a bookshop selling fancy goods,
like statues of Our Lady.
The 'Erris' was a high class joint,
in Castle Lane's heyday, Castle Lane's heyday.

The big people would gather in,
to Pat Lavelle the Saddler.
They'd sit around a warm turf fire,
full of tae, full of 'blather'.
We never knew what the stories meant,
it was all a grown-up mystery.
I heard 'Leather' and 'Greyhounds'
mentioned there and ancient Irish history.
Ancient Irish history.

The children charged down the lane
to spend a little copper.
They'd buy a slab, a sailor's chew, a
bullseye or a gobstopper.
It was a proper torture after school,
all I had was a silver tanner.
May would help us what to choose,
and I'd wish that I was thinner.
I'd wish that I was thinner.

Growing up on Castle Lane,
there was music all around me.
Pianos, cellos, violins, Pearse C and
Stephen Garvey.
My mother danced the 'Blackbird'.
I hummed the 'Foggy Dew'.
Christy sang light opera.
He starred in *The Mikado*.
He starred in *The Mikado*!

Every Sunday at one o'clock,
my heroes would assemble.
From the barracks would pound the F.C.A.
The street would shake and tremble.
'Clé, Deis, Clé', to Ludden's house
for a feed that was truly savage.
Then they'd fight amongst themselves.
Full of bacon, spuds and cabbage.
Full of bacon, spuds and cabbage.

All has changed on Castle Lane.
We're all now Europeans!
Men in Brussels call the shots, it makes me
want to scream. We've got Bistros now,
and Pound shops too, buskers playing polkas.
Unisex hair salons that have never
heard of Brylcream. Never heard of
Brylcream.

I suppose it's all for the best,
I wish each one goodwill.
Still today I feel quite sad
when I picture it in the old days.
Castlebar is growing up.
I'm thirty years in Brisbane.
But I'm glad I saw it in its heyday,
a world called Castle Lane, a world called Castle Lane.

Notes on the song:
One fateful day in spring, I sat in a café in Castle Lane, Castlebar and started writing. I imagined what it was like in 1954, and I remembered what it was like growing up in the street in the late '50s and through the '60s. They say songs are made, just waiting to appear. It was like that with 'Castle Lane, Castlebar'. The story and the tune came together, and I will always treasure the song. When I sing it, I sometimes add or subtract, depending on the form. Things have changed on Castle

Lane, we've gone pure mental. Head shops, downtime, takeaways and Pound shops...

Mattie Lennon, my friend from Wicklow, wrote in *Ireland's Own* in 2001:

> *Castle Lane is where John was born, reared and grew up. He still walks on, and loves the street. So evocative is this work that you can almost hear the tramp of the L.D.F [Local Defence Force] boots. And with any stretch of the imagination your mental nostrils will be assailed by the smell of freshly cured bacon and new leather from the saddler's. It's a tribute to the auld stock of Castlebar and a lot of other places too. It also recaptures a distant youth in song.*

On My Side

(John Hoban)

Tell me what I need to know, I'm willing to change I'm letting go.
I want to be like a stream down a mountain side.
You give to me everything I need,
I don't mind the pain or how I bleed.
When the day is done, you are on my side.

You are on my side since time began,
you loved me grow from child to man.
Even through the days I didn't want to know,
how great it is to swim in the sea,
to watch the fishermen on the quay,
laugh and tell me they were on my side.

(Chorus)
I knew no other way,
nor the price I had to pay,
for clinging to the past,
with no surrender.
I was blind but now I see
the truth inside of me.
No matter how I go,
you're on my side.

I'm grateful for the chance to know,
who I am in each friend and foe.
I see my own reflection in their eyes,
these growing pains are teaching me,
love, truth and serenity.
When the day is done,
you are on my side.

You are on my side through thick and thin.
In Asia Minor, I learned to swim,
I danced through the streets of Efes long ago,
I lit a candle in Mary's house,
met two friends inside the Blue Mosque.
Through all these great events you are on my side.

Notes on the song:
This song came about in Turkey, Kuşadasi, in 1989. It's all true and the start of the song reflects my first memories of sitting out on the shores of Dubh Loch, in County Mayo, probably in the late '50s, looking at the mountains and the rivers and streams. Feeling so connected to nature and to the Creator. A great, great time. Next thing, I was on a pier in Kadıköy in Istanbul, watching a few fishermen clowning around. They invited me into their company. I didn't know a word they were saying, but I felt we were all connected. I felt the world, everything, was on my side.

On then to Efes, Kuşadasi, and Mary's house in Selçuk in Asia Minor. It's all in the song. It's about my life, the true story. All of it is meant to be exactly as it is, and was. The song celebrates that fact. 'You are on my side through thick and thin...'

Chapter 2

HOME – MUSIC, SONG, DANCE

Music is the best medium for awakening the soul;
there is none better.
Music is the shortest, the most direct way to God,
but one must know what music is and how to use it.
(Sufi Inayat Khan)

'Home' is a big word. I heard a man in San Francisco say, "Home is when you're there, no one can put you out." I wonder? Óró 'sé do bheatha abhaile' (welcome home). It was in Glide Memorial Church that I heard a man speak about 'home'. The themes of home and homelessness have been a major part of my music and my life. For the first sixteen years of my life, Wesport Road, Castlebar, was my home. After my parents passed away in 1967 (my mother) and 1970 (my father), home was mostly temporary – lodgin' houses, flats and squats all over the place. Sometimes I even slept out.

However, the idea of home for me has always been spiritual in essence. It feels like being part of something, a sense of belonging. Music feels like home to me, it has done since day one. I don't know if describing music as my home is suitable or correct, but I do know that music gives me a sense of belonging and acceptance, no matter where I am at any given time.

Music, a sound or song, a bird singing, a saxophone playing, Cooley, Coltrane or Chopin? I don't know. The feeling is there, the heart starts beating, the tear in the eye appears and the foot starts tapping. Sometimes it's just wonderful singing a song for a few people, or playing a waltz on the melodeon. Home boys, home. A longing maybe, or else it's just this, just now, home at last, the feeling deep down.

West of our home on the Westport Road lay The Reek, the sacred mountain/pyramid on which St. Patrick fasted for 40 days and 40 nights (and drove all the snakes out of Ireland). St. Mary's

13

psychiatric hospital, known to us as 'The Mental', lay to the east, a home to hundreds of inmates with whom I felt a very definite connection. 'The Mental' was a local term used for the hospital, not very complimentary, and certainly not politically correct by today's standards, however, this is what it was known as when I was a boy. I sang in the church choir, and we sang in the awful rooms of St. Mary's at various times of the year. I loved to visit 'The Mental' with my father delivering groceries to the canteen. The patients were always cadging tobacco from us kids so they could make their own cigarettes wrapped up in *The Connaught Telegraph*. My grandfather and my godfather also worked in St. Mary's.

I served Mass and sang in the tiny chapel on the summit of Croagh Patrick. We felt raised 'up on eagles' wings', holy as could be, angels. A tough auld climb but hey, it's worth it for the view. 365 islands in Clew Bay, believe it or not.

Normal living, school, everywhere (except on a football field), felt difficult, and I got to know the four horsemen: Terror, Bewilderment, Frustration and Despair. They were always hovering around me and within me. Music, football, daydreaming and prayer were home or salvation to me. Comfort – presence and defense – music was my lifeline, the key of the door to the world I loved and trusted; the wooden, beautiful sounds from the 'wireless' radio.

One Christmas, as I spun the dial, I came across Phil and Don Everly singing 'Let It Be Me'. I also hit on Elvis singing Junior Parker's 'The Mystery Train' as I watched the lights of the Dublin-Westport train flash through Gilmartin's hazlewood, Ballymacragh, and on out to Cabbage Town. The radio was a true friend, a wise old sage. Dermot fixed it when it broke. He was a genius. Over a long dark evening, it was great to flick and visit Hilversum, Prague, Athlone, Moscow, Hank Williams, Son House, Howlin' Wolf and the classics. I loved all the music. No boundaries at all, at all.

The beauty of music is that it is both the source of creation and the means of absorbing it. (Sufi Inayat Khan)

I feel the whole idea of imposing boundaries around music destroys the creative process. I can only speak for myself. I don't believe there is such a thing as rock'n'roll, folk, jazz, classical, etc. I sometimes use these terms, but I don't believe they really exist as a concept. A lot of older traditional musicians played and sang everything without questioning which flag it falls under. I was so happy to sing Jimmy Rodgers' songs ('The Singing Brakeman') with two of the greatest fiddle players in the history of Irish music, Andy McGann and Máirtín Byrnes. They both loved to yodel, and, they both loved all types of music, 'so long as it's good music', as they would say. I'm sure all true musicians are the same. It's the feeling. It's the flavour.

Our family outings long ago, the road trips in the wagon, were a howl. We were like the Von Trapp family, the Carter family, a happy family singing in harmony. There are eight of us today. Máire passed away as a baby in the 1940s. Now we have Anne, Brendan, Carmel, Sheila, Maria, Ber and Claire (and of course me). All lovely singers, dear hearts and gentle people. The family, my mother, father, sisters and brother, always sang. Each person had, still has, a song or two they can be identified with. To this day, each one of the family sings their heart out and music plays a major part in each one's life. I seem to be the only one who plays fiddles and the banjo etc., I don't understand why. However, I feel I got great help from my family in the early years in developing the love of all kinds of music, harmony, and individual expression in music and song. It all stood me well in later years.

That was my brother Silvest!
What's he got?
A row of forty medals on his chest.
(Traditional)

Some of the older family members went to piano lessons which somehow petered out. As we travelled over the Sheaffry hills, we sang and listened to the radio playing 'Eine kleine Nachtmusik'! Then the rosary and the trimmings, mumbling the five sorrowful mysteries looking out at Clew Bay or acres of purple and yellow flowers. All life was Schubert's *Lilac Time*, Delia Murphy's 'If I Were a Blackbird', Victor Borge's (the Danish comedy man/pianist) light opera.

Maria brought home The Byrds' 'Mr. Tambourine Man' and 'Eight Miles High'. I think she had to return the record the next day to Kilkelly's music shop because the songs were about psychedelia and LSD and bad things. Sounded fierce interesting to this kid. Far out man, tune in, turn on and lead out. I was on my way out for sure.

The back garden of a Sunday night afforded me the possibility of hearing the sounds wafting over from the famous Royal Ballroom. Chuck Berry, The Beach Boys, The Stones, rock'n'roll. I was no fan of second-class copies of U.S. country music. I loved The Freshmen's 'A Whole Lotta Love'. I suppose it was an awakening or a real spiritual/musical experience. Standing out on an August night, stars everywhere, my elder sisters gone dancing to the Royal, me hearing the sounds of the bands, the electric guitar, wondering, longing.

I used to kick football in the Royal Ballroom with a few friends, Noel J and a few lads from the Avenue. Football and music. It was called indoor football. As a young lad kicking a football around the Green or The Mall, I used to wonder why the other lads gave up so easily; why they took a break for a smoke, or why they fecked off home before the final whistle. I used to think to myself: *Do they not realise this football game is life or death? Do they not realise that this is more important than anything, even the World Cup final?* I was maybe ten years of age at the time, and a right good footballer. Dangerous, but good, all or nothing, one hundred per cent was my battle cry.

Sunday night was showtime.
In the T.F. they all took the floor.
Dark suits and the whiff of cheap perfume
drifted past our front door.
I stood in the garden, at the back of our house,
I heard rock'n'roll in the key of C.

Chuck Berry for hours,
I gazed at the stars.
It was my first escape from me.

Jesus we were innocent.
Full of wonder and awe
at the plough and the stars,
the snow on The Reek,
and the moon behind the hill.
('Innocent', John Hoban)

Stephen Garvey was a famous musician and band leader from Castle Lane, Castlebar. He used to visit our home until 1958, when he left and went to live in Texas. His music-playing felt like a wonderful gift as we sat on the dining room floor of our home, looking up at this musician in his white tuxedo playing the hits of the day, just for us. He died in Houston, Texas in the mid-1960s. They brought him home in the '90s, and I was glad to be there when his body was re-interred in Castlebar. God be good to him.

My favourite (and main) LP was Pete Seeger's *Live in Carnegie Hall*, (1963); songs sung by Pete *and* the audience – first time an audience was 'miked up'.

My father was a great storyteller, regularly freaking me out with ghost stories of Siogaí, little women appearing out of nowhere, headless dogs, pigs and spirits in and around Dubh Loch. He pointed out Famine burial sites, bleached bones of those poor people who died of hunger in the 1800s. I hear them cry still and I sing and play for them. They are hungry still, so they need songs and music.

You have heard our sighs, sometimes at night,
we are your Famine dead.
('Gross Ille', John Hoban, Vincent McGrath)

My father was a great man to visit houses and places for the chat and the tae. One place I loved was Jim and Annie's in Leitir

Broc. It was the first place I experienced live music on the accordion and fiddle. After a generous feed of calley (new potatoes, scallions and the yella salty butter and parsley), the floor was cleared for a dance. It was so wonderful. One of the songs I associate with that era is:

> *That grand cailín in her gown of green,*
> *she's the rose of Aranmore. (Traditional)*

Bridie Gallagher was a big star in those days. At home the record collection was growing (as I was) and becoming more interesting.

I heard about Civil Rights, Dr. King, Montgomery, Alabama and Rosa Parks, 'If you miss me at the back of the bus, you can find me nowhere. Come on over to the city jail, I'll be roomin' right there'. This record and these songs changed me, changed everything. I knew I'd be a singer, or something like that. 'My age it means nothing, my name it means less', 'Come all you young rebels and list while I sing', Bob Dylan and Dominic Behan. I heard somewhere that Bob Dylan got the tune for 'With God on Our Side' from listening to Dominic Behan's rendition of 'The Patriot Game' in a London club.

My brother Brendan sang 'Kevin Barry' really well. He still is, of course, a fine singer. A few years later I also heard Leonard Cohen sing 'Kevin Barry' in the National Boxing Stadium in a leather jacket, with a bass player and a small crowd at him. He said he learned the song from his grandmother who used to read W.B. Yeats to him as a child in Montreal. So now you have it.

> *I ain't scared of your jail*
> *'cause I want my freedom.*
> *(Traditional)*
> * * *
> *In Mountjoy jail, one Monday morning,*
> *high upon a gallow's tree,*
> *Kevin Barry gave his young life*
> *for the cause of liberty.*
> *(Traditonal)*

18

INNOCENT

(John Hoban)

I've been around the world and a few other places,
I'm forty-odd years of age.
I'm a nomad, an artist, a pilgrim, a fiddler,
a genuine refugee.
I've crawled cross the desert of southern Lebanon,
I swam in the Aegean sea.
But Castlebar in the County Mayo,
is home for a singer like me.

Growing up in Castlebar,
was hard going for me.
I dreamt of Valparaiso, Tibet, Yki-ki!
I dreamt of playing for the reds,
or in Croke park with the Mayo team,
but maybe next time around, le cúnamh Dé,
I'll be back as a hazel tree.

Anyways, in all fairness,
I had to get away.
I had to sing those redemption songs,
in chains in Botany Bay.
I had to sleep rough in Camden Town,
to sing out in the White Hart.
To near die of thirst, to live high and low,
to get back to the County Mayo.

(CHORUS)
Jesus, we were innocent.
Full of wonder and awe
at the plough and the stars,
the snow on The Reek,
and the moon behind the hill.

My godfather worked in 'The Mental',
my grandfather was a keeper there too.
I always wanted to see number 9,
to smoke tea leaves in *The Mayo News*.
I loved the men and the women,
who lived there and visited our home.
They were gentle and kind and true to me,
as I wandered through the fields on my own.

Saturday night we were under siege,
for the 'Kraylem Navy' hit town.
They were full of poitín and diabhlaíocht
stuff us gasúrs should not know.
Linenhall Street was lined with bikes,
with 'the messages' still tied on the back.
The ham and tomato for 'the priest's tea',
cards of chocolate for the gasúrs at home.

Sunday night was showtime.
In the Royal, they all took the floor.
The smell of dark suits and cheap perfume,
drifted past our front door.
I stood in the garden,
at the back of our house,
heard rock'n'roll in the key of C,
Chuck Berry for hours,
I gazed at the stars,
it was my first escape for me.

The very first crime committed,
we were all of nine or ten.
We ducked into the Protestant church,
our very first mortal sin.
We knew then we'd all
fry forever in hell,
we were now on the run for sure,
outlaws, desperados, wanted men,
just gasúrs having a bit of fun.

Smoking was a great pastime.
We'd no truck with na cailíní at all.
If the truth were known,
they terrified us.
Them and their silly goings on.
Games of football on The Mall,
went on for days on end.
I recalled first hearing Dylan singing,
that song 'Blowing in the Wind'.

'No more auction block for me,
many thousands gone'.

We smoked Woodbine and Sweet Afton,
Park Drive and the butt of a Player.
We bought them, shaking off Delia,
mitching from school,
on the tear.
We smoked them in the graveyard,
got sick and threw up in the lake.
Between the jigs, reels and the Silvermints,
I was living like a lowdown snake.

Gilmartin's wood was paradise,
we camped there,
I was Robin Hood.
The fuscia, hazel nut and blackberries,
we gathered in a shiny tin can.
We brought them home to the women,
who made tarts and blackberry jam.
We made bows and arrows
from sally rods,
to fight off the 'bogeyman'.

My very first day in school I recall,
was a total disaster for me.
All I could see, in a room full of kids,
was a hobbyhorse sneerin' at me.
We were told 'stand there for the present.'
I broke down and was carted off home.
When they finally found out,
what was bothering me,
they never gave me the present, d'ya see.

We listened to Radio Luxembourg,
under the covers at night.
Céilí House and *The Waltons* played
the songs our fathers couldn't stand.
Fr. Shannon taught us well,
the art of harmony.
Mother Lawrence taught us to count,
A haon, dó, trí.

Notes on the song:
A long drawn out account of the innocence of growing up.
It is all there, music, football, The Davitt's, Pearse's, McHale's
and Emmett's, the 'Shop', Castle Lane, Loch Lannagh, 'The
Mental', the Church and so on...a haon, dó, trí...

GROSS ILLE

(John Hoban with Vincent Mc Grath)

I was born in Ireland in the year 1820,
in a village near the border
of Galway and Mayo.
I was married with three children,
the potato crop failed us.
Saw my brothers and sisters,
die painfully slow.

The pangs of this hunger
took hold of my people.
Saw them die by the roadside,
the young and the old.
We had heard of a place,
you now call Canada,
where we could live,
with dignity and hope,
we were told.

Said goodbye to my parents,
I'd never again see them,
with my wife and three children,
we left Liverpool by sea.
We thought we had left
the horror behind us,
on a ship called *The Syria*,
we met death and disease.

In my arms, my wife died,
between Ireland and Canada.
Her last breath was a prayer,
she was buried at sea.
I too was dying, from starvation and sickness,
by the time our ship anchored,
at the Isle of Gross Ille.

Separated from my children,
confined to the island.
I died and was buried,
on the sacred new land.

I ask now that our graves,
be rightfully honoured,
please sing my song,
so all may understand.

This is my story,
a terrible story,
starvation midst plenty,
denied dignity or hope,
thanks to the people of Quebec and Canada
for adopting our children,
giving them a good home.

The last words I speak you,
they come from a coffin ship,
spoken by a crayture from Erris at home.
You have heard our sighs sometimes at night,
we are your famine dead.

Notes on the song:

In 1992, I first went to Windsor, Ontario, in Canada, to teach and to play music for a group of people who lived there. They called themselves The Irish Canadian Cultural Club – nothing to George O'Dowd's band in London, The Culture Club. I made friends with a lot of the people there. I became especially good friends with Vincent McGrath and his family. Agnes is his good wife. Vince and I shared a very deep, common interest in the Famine, or the Drochshaol (bad life) in Ireland in 1800 and 1847-1850. So, between the jigs and the reels, after many's the long hour and day speaking and walking, Vince recalled listening to stories about the Famine from his neighbour, an elderly woman. We took these memories and put them into song, from the Island of Gross Ille. Saol fada, Vince agus Agnes, agus freisin do bhur gclann 's bhur gcairde (long life to you and to your family and friends).

Chapter 3

NATIONAL SCHOOL –
CHOIR AND MARCHING BAND

Back through the Glen, I rode again
but my heart with grief was sore.
For I'd parted then with gallant men
I never would see no more.
To and fro in my dreams I go
I kneel and I pray for you.
For slavery fled, O glorious dead
when you fell in the foggy dew.
('The Foggy Dew', Peadar Kearney)

National school, St. Patrick's, was a proper jungle. I was clever, intelligent and to some degree streetwise from working from a very young age (against my will I may add – I only wanted to play football and to hang out on The Mall) in my father's grocery shop. I was grateful for this work experience in later life. I felt, in school, that I was always dodgin' the bullets, anticipating danger, and seeking refuge in the spirit world of music and prayer. From the grocery trade you got a good grounding in manners, people-pleasing and being what was known as a grand gasúr (good kid).

In school, big rough De La Salle brothers, mostly from Munster, tried to break our spirits. I hear them still, "Clé-deis-clé-deis" (left, right, left, right). Some of the brothers were sound enough, others were not so sound by a long shot.

My first ever solo music job was singing for a Christmas concert in the school hall, eight years of age. I sang two songs, 'The Foggy Dew' and 'The Old Woman from Wexford'. I believe I went down well as I never heard otherwise from the critics, of which there were many. Brother Augustus Caesar stood in the wings as I sang, in case I made a bags of it or in case I made a bolt for the door.

Performing and singing in public came naturally to me. I would have been quite introverted as a young lad but I vividly recall my first public solo singing event. I felt completely at home on stage, as if I *belonged* there. I loved the songs and the singing so much that I felt real and creative. Later, in secondary school, this really came to the fore in the operas. I loved the whole world of acting. I felt like a natural actor, but as soon as I left the stage I felt awkward and watched. The songs and singing have always been an integral part of me. When I am performing, I feel that I am passing my songs on, letting them go. I feel that I was born to do two things, sing and kick football. Everything else, bar prayer and meditation, was, and sometimes still is, a real trial. Life is not easy, but to sing and play it out of me seems to be the path to the deep reality, Nirvana, who knows?

Once, the Clancy Brothers (different class of brothers, rock stars really) got conferred with the freedom of the town of Castlebar. We were all there to hear them shout out 'Whiskey in the Jar' and 'Brannen on the Moor' at the courthouse. It seemed like they were Yanks because of their attire and their attitude. They hung out in Greenwich Village with Bob Dylan, Dylan Thomas and Brendan Behan in the White Horse Inn on Hudson Street. Good luck to them all.

I didn't identify with the raucous, rough stage Irishy nature of their music, but I still liked some of it. I listened close as I felt it was part of a bigger thing. It was more than just the Clancy Brothers, it was their connections to theatre and the Beat Poets in Greenwich Village (whom I loved), Tipperary, and, of course, the world of Irish America and emigration. A whole world of music and life was opening up in me and I was soaking it all up, listening and learning as if my life depended on it. I feel the same way today. I was also realising three things: music was my first language; it is was an inside job; it was also guiding, directing, teaching and comforting me on this path to God-knows-where.

The school band episode was a disaster. The selector, Brother Augustus (again), decided I had not got it in me to be a fifer, so I ended up on the bass drum. I, of course, believed his decision had something to do with my stout physique. A major resentment was carried and nursed by me for decades as I recalled the pain of parading like an eejit around McHale Park football pitch on Connacht final day. I will never forget it, Galway (*three-in-a-row men*, they had won the Connacht final three years running) versus Mayo (Jinkin' Joe and Co. – the team). I remember the tunes, 'Step Together' and 'The Mountains of Pomeroy' (two of my favourite marches). It was through this music that I began to feel a sense of closeness to Tyrone people, and to Northern people in general.

I have always felt like a traveller in the word of Irish traditional music, visiting sacred sites all around the country. The common language of music makes me feel at home everywhere. When the song in the heart stopped, or the set dance was finished, I always seemed to take to the road. Sometime long ago, in the eighth or ninth-century (maybe later, who knows?), I think I may have lived in County Tyrone and played music there. I may also have lived in Belfast and left from there for to sail the Seven Seas. Songs and traditional music make me feel that this is my truth.

My involvement in the church choir was important for me. I received great musical training and experience under the direction of Fr. Thomas. My natural spiritual way could be expressed through music, which is as good as it gets. As my friend James used to say, "Sing for High Mass, Low Mass or no Mass at all." Sing out and walk on.

I sang in the choir to learn about harmony, singing with tenors, bass, sopranos and altos. 'How Beautiful upon the Mountain', 'The Diadem', and the High Latin Mass for the dead were the best of all. I could feel the vibes, the blues. A community of song, a sacred noise, as it should be.

I was introduced to street singing, busking and beggin' while singing with the choir. I remember standing on New Line (near where my mother hailed from, Sruthan – underground stream), twenty or thirty voices singing on a freezing cold December night, between the public houses, with the smell of porter and Woodbines and the hum of conversation. All the music – four-part harmony – was taught to us 'by ear' as they say. The priest, Fr. Tom, or the organist, Seán, played the phrase on the organ, and each part of the choir learned their line. It was a great introduction to singing and making music with others. It was also very well received and well respected by audiences. I loved it totally.

Castlebar in the late '50s and the early '60s was a much quieter place in which to grow up; there were not so many cars, and there was a lot less hustle and bustle compared to today. I recall hearing people, tradesmen especially, whistling beautifully as they went about their daily business. Whistling a Buddy Holly song, 'Peggy Sue' maybe, or 'Rose of Mooncoin', or 'La Paloma'. These were the songs our fathers would have loved. Beautiful, bird-like whistling. You don't hear them at it anymore. Is mór an trua é (It's a great pity). The auld stock could do it for sure.

We sang all over the town and, on Christmas day, we sang our hearts out in 'The Mental' and in the workhouse, to those sacred hearts who lived there, some under lock and key. 'Hosanna in the Highest, Hosanna in the Highest'.

CHRISTY WAS A COVIE

(John Hoban)

Christy was a Covie,
make no mistake about it.
Grew up in Carrabán,
served his time to the grocery trade.
He lived a while in Glasgow,
in the Gorbals in the '30s.
Returned to the 'old sod',
when he felt he had it made.

The kids grew up right on the edge,
they were neither town nor country.
They played Gaelic for the Emmet's,
soccer for Celtic on the sly.

They played handball in 'The Mental',
with the patients and their keepers,
played hurling on Lough Lannagh,
it frozen solid, I recall.

(Chorus)
Níl aon tinteán mar do thinteán féin
There's no hearth like your own hearth.
Níl aon tinteán mar do thinteán féin,
all aboard the mystery train.

Each Sunday after chicken dinner,
they'd load up the silver wagon,
like cowboys, pilgrims, pioneers,
they'd head West out to The Reek.

They'd sing, they'd argue,
they'd listen to the radio,
Micheál Ó hEithir would announce to all,
'Dia daoibh, a chairde go léir.'
They'd cross the creek into town,
they'd greet all Christy's cronies,
Brodie, lived on Shop Street,
played snooker in the town hall.

The big treat was ten ice creams,
from B. Hyland on this wooden tray.
Then on to visit Sally,
saying the rosary all the way.

Dada Hodie read 'the truth in the news'.
Sarah came from Coisloch,
on the day of the famous ambush,
they were burned out by the Tans.

The old people spoke in whispers,
about the Battle of the Pound.
The dreaded Houston clearances,
and the Sheaffry headless hound.

Next we went to visit by The Quay,
the kindly people who lived there.
Tea, cakes and then outside,
Tommy taught us how to play.

He starred for Connacht in both codes,
The Railway Cup as they used to say.
The Quay was a homely spot,
by the shores of dear Clew Bay.

Garland Friday they climbed The Reek,
served Mass on top, so to speak,
visited the graves at Aughvale,
then home to Castlebar.

Sin é an scéal fadó, fadó.
The story of a Sunday in West Mayo.
Christy was a Covie,
make no mistake about it.

Notes on the song:
Christy, my father, died when I was young, sixteen years of
age. We got on well, still do. He loved Westport, he was a 'Covie' (local slang for a native of Westport). Every Thursday and
Sunday he went there to visit and to 'do jobs'. This song, which
is quite recent, is from an eleven-year-old ladeen's viewpoint. A
good, humorous, honest recalling of a Sunday, every Sunday,
boiled chicken and peas, the rosary, the radio, on tour in our
wagon, the whole clann. A bit like a rock band, a road trip.

THE WESTPORT SONG –
HE CAN'T TURN IT LIKE ME

(John Hoban)

I wonder what class of a day it'll be?
I'll saunter up James Street to see who I'll see.
The horse show is on in Lord Sligo today.
There'll be crowds from Liscarney and further away.
Women are better than men on a horse.
I'll look into Sargey, he's open of course.
There's music tonight up with John McGing.
The people of High Street and John's Row can sing.

Pat Friel is playing in Clarke's all day,
P.T. Malynn is humming away.
Here comes Mr. Hoban his banjo in tow,
it's too early yet to knock up the show.
A glass of stout and a pipe of tobacco,
will do us no harm if we leave it at that.
There's rain on The Reek, a storm in Clew Bay.
I'll drop into The West for a strong cup of tae.

There's Norm, Malcolm, John Fadgin 'idithin',
Padraic and Toebar have gone for a spin.
Timber and turf make a great blaze.
The women of Ireland are going through a phase,
we can say 'Hello, how's the going?'
But there never can be any mixing with them,
you're better off single and fancy free,
than married for life in Renvyle by the sea.

Here come a few French, they are not great at the talk,
more from Clare Island, I know by their walk.
You surely heard Billy, he's tops on the box.
Have you seen Connie singing the 'Little Red Fox'?
It's five past eleven, I'm homeless once more.
I've broken the curfew, the bolt's on the door.
'You're always welcome' sez Barbara and Anne,
Sticks Geraghty's house is a far better plan!

A day in a life in County Mayo,
where they say all are welcome,
the friend and the foe.
As long as we're spared to sing out our song,
the day of the capóg
might not be gone.
Experiencin' life in County Mayo,
where merchants and serpents,
come and they go.
There's one who's outstanding,
no matter what's said,
he wears his cap the left side of his head.

Notes on the song:
The man I wrote this song about is one James O'Malley. A
great friend and musician. I wrote these words in a café in Free-
mantle, Western Australia, in 1988. The air I sing this song to is
called 'The Black Rogue'. Each line is a song in itself. As I was
writing, I kept hearing James's words, his philosophy. So, most
of the song is made up of sayings and observations he made and
shared with me over the years. James wore his cap at such a
precarious angle on the left side of his head, that he was known
as 'the man who walks beside his cap'.

Chapter 4

SECONDARY SCHOOL

St. Jarlath's College, Tuam, at that time,
was a pretty rough old station.
On bread and water we did five years,
not one of us had the vocation.
('Slán Le Van', John Hoban)

As we 'look back on life's troubled sea', St. Jarlath's years were all about opera, drama, football, sean-nós, rock'n'roll, prayer and friendship – and a fair dash of torture and confusion. My memories from this time bring me Gilbert and Sullivan, light opera, Fr. Tom and Fr. Charles, and great times for me on stage. No bother, free to act and sing. I remember being selected as the leading lady in the opera as there were no ladies to be seen in Jarlath's. The lassies nearest to us attended the Presentation and Mercy convents, separated from us by the imposing cathedral. So there was I, hitting the high notes, dancing the fandango, showing off and learning all the time. Who'd have thought I'd be starring as a lady in an opera called *The Gondoliers* at thirteen years of age?

I recall thinking that opera felt like life itself. I loved the coming together of the drama, theatre, and the sounds of the songs and music. I think of these things as being as natural as a yew tree, or a cut of brown bread and jam for that matter. It is all about natural expression. I love to think about these things.

I don't really know what my ideas were about music in those days, except that I experienced music as being somehow godlike. Music was the real world. It didn't matter where it came from or what it was called. What mattered was the feeling of the song and the way I felt listening to it. A lot of the time, I hadn't a clue what the meaning of the words were, but that didn't seem to matter to me. I remember listening to Edith Piaf without having one word of French, but loving the music all the same. Miles

Davis's jazz, Séamus Ennis on the pipes, or anything from *La Bohème* – it all came down to the feeling, the atmosphere it created. Music is my own personal, loving, inspirational sound that understands me. When I look back over my life, I can see with clarity that music has often guided me, helped me to live and love, to transcend the suffering that often arises in life.

The public performances in the town theatre at Christmas were great fun. It was like being at the Oscars in Hollywood. I just knew I was singing to save my life. The school was famous for two things, football, and the yearly opera. I was very fortunate to be good at both, and could more than pass myself with the books, even though I had no real interest in any of the subjects being taught. My passions were music and football. The only subjects I learned anything about were Latin and French because they were taught by a great teacher, Fr.Thomas. He had a love for these languages which helped me to learn. Fr. Thomas was also the director of the operas and this may have influenced my regard for him.

I don't regret the past, but I sometimes feel that the years spent sitting in classrooms were a total waste of time for me. The only time I felt excited about school was when a teacher shared his own love of learning through a subject close to his own heart. For example, when Fr. Tom taught the French language, he closed the book, and then his eyes, and spoke to us about Albert Camus or Gide or Sartre. I loved watching him take off. It was only then that I truly felt I was learning. It felt like music, belting it out. Every single one of the other so-called teachers was just reading from a book, bored with the subject, trying to pass the time, and showed no interest in who we were or where we were at.

Irish language and culture, including music, were lost to me in school, mainly due to the brutal method of teaching these subjects. In fact, it was so brutal that I dodged them as much as I could while in school. The main effect of this poor teaching was that as children, we (and me for sure), were completely turned away from the study or love of our culture, the language in particular. We received no encouragement or support from our teachers to enable us to see, or even vaguely understand, how much Irish could enrich our souls. It was awful. Fortunately this all changed for me when I met 'The Connemaras', the real deal, while in exile in Camden Town. These men gave me master classes in the language throughout the '70s, on building sites, in cafés and of course, in the tavern – the university of my life.

I couldn't wait to get away from the torture of school, both national and secondary. So for sure, only for music and the endless kicking of a football, I would have gone stone mad, or done some serious damage. Meeting up with the native Irish speakers in London gave me back a part of myself that I had lost or had learned to despise. I love the Irish language, and I came back to it through the jigs and the reels, the slides and polkas, the slow airs and the hornpipes I heard after I hit London town.

After all my great education in Mayo and Galway, isn't it hilarious to report that I learned Irish music and Irish language deep in the heart of London town. So much for *Bullaí Mháirtain* agus *Dialann Deoraí*, two dull books we were given to study in secondary school.

In Jarlath's, I had a great friend, Michael Duignan, who introduced me to Jimi Hendrix, 'Hey Joe', 'Purple Haze', 'Astral Weeks', and Chuck Berry.

Mickey D was his name, twelve bar blues was his game.
He never did achieve the fame.
As in his native land, it was riddled with c & w
so he fecked off to Iran to live. C'est la Vie.
('Mickey Dee', John Hoban)

Onwards and downwards we went, what with football, prayer, cheap altar wine and dreamtime, Dunmore McHales, tatie hokin', duckin' and divin', yes Father, no Father, when I grow up Father, I don't know Father.

There came a stage when I couldn't wait for my life to begin. This period came after both my parents had passed on after their time on earth. God be good to them. I hadn't yet started to play guitar or any instrument at this stage, that came as soon as I left school in 1970.

One night in particular stands out in my memory of secondary school. I was somehow selected as lead vocalist in a rock'n'roll outfit in a concert. Lead, bass, drums, and me. Creedence Clearwater Revival and, thankfully, 'Johnny B. Goode' helped me. This concert had a huge effect on me. I don't remember any other gig in school; this was a once-off event. On the whole, secondary school was a time for football, and a lonely sort of a feeling that we were somehow isolated from the rest of the universe.

A great friend of mine during all those times was a fíor Ghaeil (a true Irish man), Colm or Colman or Ted as he called himself, Lame Deer (Colm came from a place called Tír an Fhia, the land of the deer), corner-back, hard as nails, bright as any star in heaven. We shook hands on the last day of school, and hit for John Bull, Blighty, the mines in Wales and the squats of North London. Many moons later, we met once again in Galway. I was busking on a banjo in Shop Street, trying to hustle up the 'entrance fee' (street slang for having enough money to sit in a pub or club and buy a drink, or maybe something to eat, to show respect for the bean an tí – woman of the house, and to continue playing indoors). A tenner, sterling, fluttered into the 'hata', I looked up and saw my mate, Colm. Off we went to a fleadh cheoil (music festival) in Woodford, East Galway, for days of fun, gallons of porter, and sean-nós, old style songs. We then went our separate ways, never again to meet, in this world anyway.

Colm's first language was Irish. He sometimes spoke to me in his native tongue. I understood him and he understood where I was at. I recall seeing him sitting on a bridge in Woodford during the time of the fleadh cheoil, eyes closed, listening to Pat, Peter and Vincent Broderick play pipes and flute, and me on bouzouki, Patsy Tuohy's and John Doran's music. It was the last time I met my mate Colm. Wherever you've gone to, a chara (my friend), it's a better place than before you docked. I learned a lot beside you, and I often thank God our names fell next to each other in that vulgar system known as seniority.

Nowadays, as is often the case when I sing or play, I call on those people and those times to help me, to walk alongside the flowing river, by my side. When I am playing or singing, I often imagine a whole slua ('slew'), a communion of saints and sinners or a choir singing, playing and dancing their hearts out to the sound of the music. The music which I always do my best to give away to others.

My heart is full of gratitude for the great gift of music. My experience in the operas helped me to live, to survive the hard times, and it also prepared me, in no small way, for a life of music. For the 'Ministry of Music', my home.

He never learned to read or write too well,
but he could play the guitar
just like ringing a bell.
('Johnny B. Good', Chuck Berry)

SLÁN LE VAN

(John Hoban)

Junior Wells opened the show,
decked out in a purple suit.
He sang and leapt around the stage,
the man didn't give a hoot.
The Chicago sound of rhythm and brass,
blew me right away,
'Good morning little school girl,'
from Sonny Boy showed the way.

Van came out like a full force Gael,
asked 'did you get the feeling?'
I got it alright, down to my soul,
I was back on the old sod kneeling.
St. Jarlath's College, Tuam,
at that time,
was a pretty rough old station.
On bread and water we lived five years,
not one of us had a vocation.

Then one night we heard 'Moondance',
it took away all the pain.
We listened close to the radio,
nothing was ever the same.
School shut down, we were on the road.
Met Madame George on the Appian Way,
squatted in London in '73,
'til I woke to a brand new day.

All through the '70s and '80s,
all through the darkest days,
Tupelo Honey and Domino,
lightened up our ways.
I once took a train from Dublin town,
right up to the Sandy Row.
Cried on Cypress Avenue,
'Baby, please don't go.'

Back in San Francisco,
December '93,
Van is singing with Junior Wells,
another homecoming for me.
Jimmy Witherspoon, Georgie Fame.
The band are really having a blast.
We're on our feet screaming Gloria,
right now there is no past.
There is no future, no tomorrow,
it's always been right now.
Thanks my friend for being around,
too late to stop now!

Notes on the song:
December 1993, I found myself *on tour* in the USA. I had
finished my work teaching and playing in Windsor, Ontario,
Canada. I had also made a few trips across the border to Detroit, to meet and play with the friendly sons and daughters of
Erin, Michigan, Lebanon and all other points. Easy-wandering
around Motown always turned me on musically. Detroit, was
one helluva town and very significant in my life, as was San
Francisco. So, here I am busking outside the Masonic Temple
on Nob Hill, greeting a crowd of Van Morrison fans (who is to
do a concert 'idithin' – inside). After playing my jigs, reels and
singing 'Cypress Avenue' and 'Oh! The Water', in I go, having
made a fair few bucks. I could not believe my luck, or the music
I was hearing.

One of my heroes in music at this time was Junior Wells. There he was up on the stage, backed by an eight-piece band of Chicago heads, decked out in an exquisite purple suit, eighty-plus years of age, belting out some of the finest music I have ever heard. The man, Van, came on afterwards and he too was wonderful. I had flashbacks to the early '70s in Dublin, Belfast and London, listening to his latest records. They helped me limp along through good times, hard times and blank times. For this, I was grateful to Van Morrison, his songs, and once more to the gift of music itself.

The next day, I was strolling around The Mission District of San Francisco when a real beauty of a melody came together with a song in my head. I went into a music instrument shop (a sort of pawn shop for guitars), and pretended to buy a guitar as I worked out my 'Slán (farewell) to Van'. I hope he's keeping well and healed – 'It's too late to stop now...' I always dedicate 'Slán Le Van' to my good friend Sharon Shannon. Our paths crossed in 1988, I believe, and we are still trudgin' the broad highway. She continues to be a true friend, a wonderful musician, and a connection through sound and music that makes sense when nothing else does. Wherever she is, it's really only a song or a tune away. Same as a thought or a prayer, or a shadow running across the Diamond Mountain in spring.

AS GOOD AS IT GETS

(John Hoban)

There's just no way to say all that I feel,
for you, in this song.
Then again this love makes us both feel as one, so real,
so incredibly true.
Time passing by leaves a tear in the eye,
as I sit here at home missing you.
I'm so glad that I lived, glad that I felt,
every single second loving you.

We know what it's like to love and be loved,
in this life, that's as good as it gets.
It's real hard to let go,
but as always you show that our love
is as good as it gets.

Now you've moved on, your spirit is free,
like an eagle to shine and to soar.
Of course, I miss madly a thousand things about you,
your presence standing at my door.
Now we're together for ever and ever,
hearts heal with timeless wonder.
Each day I keep finding deeper reminders,
of loving you, a ghrá, precious you.

Notes on the song:
Written in Mount Melleray, a Cistercian abbey in Waterford,
Ireland. 2008. A friend's husband passed away and I wanted to
write a song from her perspective, but it could also be the other
way around. Eternal love.

Chapter 5

EXILE, DUBLIN, THE '70S

If ever you go to Dublin town
In a hundred years or so,
Inquire for me in Baggot Street
And what I was like to know...
(Patrick Kavanagh)

In the '60s, with no sense, I went on holiday to Dublin, staying with my eldest sister, Anne, in her flat on Waterloo Road. Compared to the demanding work in the shop back home in Castlebar, the few days in Dublin were a breeze. Dublin was a much quieter, less hostile, place in the '60s. I had no bother walking around on my own, even though I was only ten years of age. While Anne worked all day, I 'hoofed' it into town or took the number 10 bus (top deck of course) and thoroughly explored the areas around Baggot Street, the Grand Canal and Stephen's Green.

This was the era of The Beatles. I spent days listening to, and learning from, *Rubber Soul* and of course, *Revolver*. I loved the early stuff with Lennon singing rock'n'roll. Then *Sgt Pepper's* came out and it literally blew my mind.

I read the news today, oh! boy!
About a lucky man who made the grade...
('A day in the life', Lennon & McCartney)

Luke Kelly was in Dublin around this time. Later in life, I met him in a pub once, and he sang a few songs for the company. It was down in Sheriff Street and I remember him singing 'Monto', 'The Streams of Bunclody' and other songs with his mates. I felt blessed when I heard him sing live.

Just like the music showing up out of nowhere, the poetry and the person of Patrick Kavanagh got a hold of me early on in my life. They somehow found me without me looking for them. I love the poetry and writing of Rainer Maria Rilke, William Blake, Rabindranath Tagore, Albert Camus, all the Blasket Island writers, but Patrick Kavanagh tops them all.

Patrick Kavanagh lived near my sister's flat. One day, a man pointed him out to me. Kavanagh was leaning over Baggot Street Bridge, looking into the green, mossy canal. He was wearing a big long tweed coat and a hat on his head. I was only a young boy so I didn't say hello. My man said to me, "There is the best poet in Ireland." He is that to me for sure.

Sometime in the mid-'70s, I found myself standing in the Phoenix Bar in Dundalk, not quite sure how I got there or what I was doing there. Two ladies were behind the bar, Rita and her mother Katie. I can't remember how the conversation began, but in no time there were two main topics, Patrick Kavanagh and Clare Island, County Mayo. Katie Winters came from Clare Island, and Rita knew Kavanagh very well and said it was very sad that he and I had never met. She felt we would have got on famously. Some weeks later, Rita introduced me to Kavanagh's hometown of Iniskeen, County Monaghan. We took a trip out there on a cold December day, walked around for a while, and stopped to play a bit of music. This journey also brought us to Kelly's in Essexford where, I believe, Paddy was always made welcome. We watched the older men play a game of pitch and toss, and even joined in for a while.

In school, a few months after returning from my holiday with my sister in Dublin, our English teacher came pounding into class and announced "Poor Paddy Kavanagh is dead." I remember it was a wet November day, 1967. We all read and listened to his poetry in the days that followed.

You flung a ditch on my vision
Of beauty, love and truth.
O stony grey soil of Monaghan,
You burgled my bank of youth!
('Stony Grey Soil', Patrick Kavanagh)

In Dublin, my sister showed me the art galleries, the Abbey Theatre and the Focus Theatre. I remember seeing Ibsen's 'A Doll's House' and a Chekov play whose title I don't recall. I loved Stanislavski's Method style of acting. I felt that I too was living life on stage and becoming a real actor myself, in my own life.

I have always felt very grateful to the people I've met along the way who helped me to see my back, or my soul, or a new world. I feel that we each have the ability to unlock doors for one another when we are connected in a spiritual sense. Anne introduced me to the world of art and theatre when I was quite young. This world immediately held my interest, and this interest soon grew to encompass the world of politics, and much more. I was only ten years of age, but I still feel I understood and loved this creative world of the 'arts'. I've never studied art, nor have I ever taken a music lesson, however, my visits to the art galleries in Dublin at this time left an indelible mark on me; this is the world in which I did my learning. The world of the arts came alive for me in the Focus Theatre and while listening to every kind of music available in the '60s. The arts shone a light into dark corners. I felt alive with a real sense of belonging, and it made me feel connected to a power much greater than me. Music, in particular, has become the filter through which I sift all information passing between my inner and outer realities, and the lens through which I see the world.

Sometimes, I feel quite certain that I have lived other lives, in other times. For example, I feel sure I lived as a musician in Efes in Turkey, a convict in Australia, a troubadour in Spain, a Cajun or maybe even a shrimp in Louisiana, and I think it is quite possible that I died in the Famine on Achill Island. I kind of know that I have lived many, many more lives besides. So there we are.

'C'est la vie', say the old folks.
Goes to show you never can tell!
('C'est la Vie', Chuck Berry)

Now, it's early 1970, I am on the train from the West, sixteen years of age, having finished my education, my schoolin'. It feels like I have no home, 'Like a Rollin' Stone' (like Muddy Waters). It feels, and looks, like exile, emigration. So, I'll have some beer in the old railway station bar in Athlone before the train leaves Connacht for the East. I feel I've set foot on 'the lost highway', but it's all there is left. Precious Lord, walk with me. The story of my life seems to be about having a certain faith in life, shown most clearly to me in music. I can't recall feeling worry or fear about the future, just going from day to day. Singing, listening and trying to stay awake and out of harm's way.

Then the bottle came into my life, bringing with it a sense of power which had been mostly missing in my life. My Life was about to take off anytime soon. 'One of these days I'll make my move...'

The kindness of my family helped me to live, and to deal somewhat with my sense of grief and loss of my home, my parents, my future, my hope and my emptiness. With the beer in Athlone, I had found a power greater than myself. This new-found power was strong, subtle, savage, cunning and baffling. Ahead of me lay seventeen years full on with this power, no turning back

Soon after arriving in Dublin, a Landola guitar comes to me and I play it until my fingers bleed, 'Hard Rain's Gonna Fall' for sure. Songs keep showing up, 'Suzanne', 'Me and Bobby McGee', 'Spancil Hill', 'Times They Are a-Changin'. Again, strangely but naturally, I feel I don't really have to learn to play. I just play and I give myself totally to the ceol (music).

I have always known that my voice, singing and speaking, is my first and primary musical instrument. I started strumming the guitar when I was sixteen, but prior to that I had a lifetime of listening to, and learning from, all kinds of sounds, songs, noises, and music. I believe that the word 'persona' comes from the Latin 'personare', meaning 'through sound' (a *persona* was also used as a mask by players in Greek theatre). I have learned that a person's voice is like an image in sound, a reflection of a person's state of being, of their soul – a barometer of the condition of their spirit. This is more apparent to me today as I listen and realise that no two voices are the same. It is so wonderful to listen to one person after another singing, regardless of the quality of the singing. The sound of each person's voice tells the truth of his or her being. Whether I like it or not, whether they like it or not, *c'est vrai* (it's true). I also notice that I am only drawn to a voice that is natural. If it is trained or elocuted, it does not sound true to me, and I can find it almost amusing. When some people sing, I find they can move me emotionally, regardless of what they are singing about. They reach a place within me that nothing else can reach. No instrument can go as deep into the soul as the voice. I have also learned that all instruments aspire to the voice. The sitar, vina, slide guitar, cello, pipes, and even the vuvuzela, all try to imitate the human voice.

I remember, some time ago, hearing a late night radio discussion about singers. The discussion was held between half a dozen eminent vocalists, each one expounding their opinions on who they thought was the greatest singer of all time. I thought it was sheer, daft madness. However, the last person to give an opinion (someone whom I like to listen to singing) came out with an original statement which I will never forget. He said, "Well, you know, I'm the best singer I've ever heard." It sounded so humorous and true.

The Hindus of ancient times said that singing was the first art, playing music the second, and dancing the third. All the great prophets of the Hindus were singers, like Narada and Tumbara. Finally, a person once told me that inspiration chooses its own voice. So, I never doubted that my primary musical instrument was, and is, my natural voice. I guess I'll be singing till the last breath is drawn, singing till the last trumpet sounds, singing my way back home.

Dublin in the early '70s seemed to be very rich with music to this boy from the West. I began my internal trudge on a twisted path from music to music, from Sweeney's Men to Rory Gallagher to the Swamp Folk Club to Alan Stivell to Johnny Moynihan, and from Joni Mitchell to Granny's Intentions, to Liam Weldon and Séamus Ennis. I was totally immersed in live music of all kinds. I heard all these people, and many others, play live. I especially loved the folk clubs, The Universal in Parnell Square, The Swamp in Rathmines, The Coffee Kitchen, and the one in The Central in Aungier Street where I heard Liam Weldon sing 'Dark Horse on the Wind'. I used to go to hear Rory Gallagher in The Boxing Stadium and, of course, he opened the door for me to explore Blind Boy Fuller, Howlin' Wolf and Elmore James – the blues.

The Traditional Music Club in Slattery's held great nights for the culchies and Dubs alike. The likes of Geordie Hanna, Tony McMahon, Joe Ryan and John Kelly also caught my fancy. I felt my whole being was just about music in those days. Learning, listening, and developing a way of living in music. It was a very exciting and creative time for me. The world of music at this time seemed to be more individual and unique, more of an intense personal experience. This changed as the 1970s rolled on. Music was becoming more of an industry, more about bands and gigs, money-making on a grand scale and, of course, it was all about who you knew. I remember feeling that the world of music was at some sort of beginning (and maybe some kind of end), or at a crossroads in 1970/1971.

My days were spent between listening to records – my friends would come back from England with all sorts of new music LPs for me – and playing the guitar and harmonica. At night, I would go to pubs, folk clubs, concerts and plain *whoopee* parties, singing my songs and listening and learning from the great music all around the city. I also spent a good deal of time playing tennis and football in the park. A simple life, living with my sisters until I moved in with the hippies in Rathmines.

I got a pound or two together from singing on Mary Street and I hitched off for Sliabh Luachra (the poor mountain of the rushes). Although I always loved the city vibe, any city (Dublin was great, playing football in the park, the Dandelion Market, films I saw, especially *Easy Rider* – saw it six times in a row – *Woodstock, Citizen Kane* etc.), I also longed to set off for the hills, the South of Ireland first, to the music I heard of Padraic O'Keefe and his pupils. Off with me to the countryside.

I slept out in a sleeping bag, me, the guitar and the book I brought, Suzuki's *Beginner's Mind*, real cool. I also read all about the Beat Poets, Kerouac, Snyder, Gregory Corso and Ginsberg, which led me on to listen to the music of that era, Coltrane, Miles, Diz, Prez and Bird. I was living my own 'on the road' experience, dozing off under the stars in Knock-na-Gree with the fiddles of Padraic, Denis 'the Weaver', Julia Clifford (whom I was later to meet in London) playing in my head and in my soul. 'Rocking the Cradle' and Ballydesmond Polkas. Mind you, I woke up feeling not great, the usual when the party's over, cold and thirsty. Ná bac leis (not to worry), on into Castleisland for the 'cure'.

Next, on to Galway and a trip that lasted for many years.

Green and red,
black and blue.
A helpless, hopeless, dreamless view.
Hear the wind blow, love,
hear the wind blow.
Bígí ciúin.
It's the way to go.
('Black and Blue', John Hoban.)

Galway was like San Francisco. The Summer of Love lasted a week in San Francisco, and then they went off home to their beds. The party in Galway lasted, for me, until 1987. The fire took a while to die down.

At this time, Galway was awash with refugees like me. There were dozens of us, all waiting for something. We were on a voyage of discovery into our world of music, acid, life, joy and madness. All of us waiting. I came across great people, too numerous to mention except, I must say, Mickey Finn and Michael Treacy, two music people with whom I felt at home.

I could be anywhere in the country, hitch-hiking was my mode of transport, and if a seat was going to Galway, I'd go there. I was wandering aimlessly a lot of the time, so, in a way, Galway was as near to a base as I had in the '70s. I felt it was the one place I would have music seven days and seven nights a week, plenty of drink, parties and people who I felt were like me. I was always made to feel welcome because I sang and played well, and had manners. I was no trouble. I had no money, but busking was cool. I recall a few days when there were eight or ten of us all busking outside Moon's on Shop Street. We made a fair few bob, but it had to cover the whole company in Mrs. Cullen's or in The Cellar. Some of us had other jobs, but most of my friends at this time were like me, playing music for survival. It was a great way to learn music, listening to each other, and each one of us a teacher to the others. It was like a commune. It all began to change after the late '70s and early '80s for various reasons. I believe change is natural for life and growth, and this was very true for me by 1987, it was time to turn it all over to the higher powers. I reached out, and sure enough, I got a seat home.

There was no money to be made in those early days. Good, hungry music, us all learning how to 'Roll on Buddy...down the line', as the old blues number advises. We busked, drank, played music and learned from each other. Some people went straight, some died, some got real famous, a few went to college, and others went home for the tea, imagine.

The sound of fiddles, boxes and pipes came closer and louder even though I was a Motown man myself. I met 'The Bucks of Oranmore' and 'Rakish Paddy', 'Bonny Kate' and 'Jenny's Chickens'. My native music led me on many journeys throughout the country. A tune like 'The Battle of Aughrim' led me to East Galway and to The Old Ballinakill and Aughrim Slopes Céilí Bands. I visited many places with my music. I remember one night in Gentian Hill in Galway, I discovered that if I sang my heart out, I'd be granted shelter. But once again, the firewater took over, loss of memory, helter skelter into a dark place.

I played the bouzouki to the great music of the Brodericks who hailed from 'The Lighthouse in the Bog' in Bullan. This house was literally a beacon for those like me passing by, imagine a farmhouse in the middle of a bog, lit up all night long, inviting us in. Down in East Galway, I heard the pipes of the Travellers, John and Felix Doran, The Cash family playing 'Col. Frazer',

'My Love is in America' and 'Sliabh na mBan'. Fairy music for sure.

I used to meet Máirtín Byrnes in McDaid's and in O'Donoghue's in Dublin. He hailed from the same country of East Galway. I knew his music from *Paddy in the Smoke* and I admired his way with music. Máirtín led me to Michael Coleman and Frank O'Higgins. Not long before he died we met up in RTÉ (in the bar) and sang and yodelled Jimmy Rodgers' songs including 'The Singing Brakeman'. I felt then Máirtín was set to go, he wore a white suit, the colour of grief. I will never forget this night. Desi Halloran, his old friend from his London days, was also in the company.

It was a *Late, Late Show* special about music and dance from the Islands. I got the call from the good people of Cliara (or Clare Island). I was living in Dublin, learning about a new life, and I was included as part of this Clare Island ensemble. We had great craic, as they say. Billy Gallagher, my good friend and great accordionist, and me on tenor banjo playing for the dancers. All descendants of Gráinne Uaile. We did our best. The Inis Bofins followed us. Afterwards, we were guests of honour in the bar and that was where Máirtín, the crayture, was sitting waiting for us. It was 1988. Máirtín passed away not long afterwards. I thank God we had that great time on that night.

Aithníonn Ciaróg Ciaróg eile (one insect recognises another). It takes one to know one, she smiled.
('Ciaróg', John Hoban)

Music was shifting me around like a pawn on a chessboard. I prayed under the stars a lot as I slept rough, sad, mad but also kinda glad. I loved to watch the sun rise, and to think about the lilies in the field beside me. As Wally Page sings, 'There's always tomorrow'. There has always been a tomorrow for me.

However, London was calling. I think the choice was made a long way back. The famous boat from Dun Laoghaire, hassle in Holyhead, train to Euston, London town, at last. So, off to Camden Town..., "Mind the doors, all change for Paddington."

BLACK & BLUE

(John Hoban)

Black 'n' blue,
green and red.
Shuffling around the street half dead.
A helpless, hopeless, dreamless view.
Green and red.
Black and blue.

Purple and brown.
Yellow and white.
Now she's skipping down the street at night.
An icy wind, a sleeping town.
Yellow and white, purple and brown.

Hear the wind blow love.
Hear the wind blow.
Bígí ciúin.
It's the way to go.

Notes on the song:
A song about this time, 1970, homeless in the hometown.
No joke, but it could be worse. It could always be worse. I also
heard 'The Harder They Come' and 'Living in Limbo' around
this time. Identified!!

DIFFERENT

(John Hoban)

We scattered the ashes of Michael Patrick Gorman,
to the four winds 'round the bay today.
The music man has moved into another classroom.
'I was never of this world,' he used to say.
He celebrated life with an innocent abandon,
of a child with a truth he couldn't hide.
His scars were his glory, as he walked and sang his story,
from day one, he was different down the line.

Nora Kilmuray, couldn't stand the pressure,
of pretending to be precious all the time.
She had six brothers and a mother,
her father was a dealer,
she was tired of saying everything was fine.
She jumped the boat to Scotland,
got lost up in the Highlands,
wrote poetry and plays to beat the band.
Her scars where her glory, as she walked and sang her story.
Suffering, being different,
down the line.

Exile and the big house, were given as the answer,
to the strange ones who wouldn't toe the line.
They sent away the singers, the artists, the dreamers,
to wander in the desert and to pine.
For a little bit of loving,
a biteen of compassion,
a chance to stand up and say 'I am'.
The scars are their glory, as we walk and sing our story.
Suffering, being different, down the line.

Notes on the song:
Our scars are our glory. They certainly tell our story. When I hit London, I thought, *So this is where they went, this is where they escaped to.* Life could now begin, the pub to the bookie to the 'room', to the café, to the job. 'You'll never go back now', I heard them say. It seemed a sad life for us all, but it was exciting too. Many of us were carrying a lot of baggage in our heads and hearts. I had no clue how to live, no roadmap, no internal reference points. The camaraderie and the sense of fellowship between exiles helped us all. We stood with, and for, each other until the grip got too tight and something had to give. I am so blessed to have lived two lives, and had a lot of different mates, many of whom never got past the first fence.

Chapter 6

THIS IS LONDON

We were born in Mayo forty years ago,
at sixteen from there we were forced go.
We took the boat to Holyhead,
lived in fear, right on the edge,
digging drains in London in the snow.
Tried to figure out how a boy became a man,
sleeping rough in the West End in a red van.
Nobody could tell me what it was all about.
So in a few short days,
we were back where we began.
('Born in Mayo' John Hoban)

L ondon was calling for sure, loud and clear. I loved the sense of being the immigrant, a kind of outcast, the men who don't fit in. The Yukon was a bit too extreme for me, I was too fond of my comforts. Kilburn, Cricklewood, the 'Dilly, Soho...the real McCoy. I had discovered anonymity, and it felt great. Sure as night follows day, I felt alive at last as the big boat, the *Bád Bán* set sail from Dun Laoghaire for Holyhead.

It was in the year of '39.
The sky was full of lead.
Hitler headed for Poland,
Paddy for Holyhead.
(Traditional)

After docking, we all boarded the trains. I remember looking at the poor souls from Connacht, sitting sad and lonely after saying their goodbyes to their people. Crying as they watched their friends and neighbours disembark at each station on that long journey to London. They drank their way to London. So did I. I also sang and felt protected by the music, my very own sound.

When the train hit Euston Station in London, I knew I was there to follow this music inside me. I had no idea how to live life on any terms. I felt a certain freedom from 'What'll the neighbours say?', *The Mayo News*, and the terror of materialism. I felt like a released prisoner, a bird set free from a cage. Little did I know what was really happening.

For a very brief time, London, the streets and the people, felt like home to me. I felt like an Indian on the prairies in those old black and white movies. Horses and horses and lots of music, lots of different people. I felt life, spiritual life, reality was now about to begin as I got into the music in every way I could. I also got into the drink, the way of life in exile. I wrote a tune to a poem by W.B. Yeats, 'An Irish Airman Forsees His Death'.

I know that I shall meet my fate
somewhere among the clouds above.
Those I fight I do not hate.
Those I guard, I do not love.

I tried the office job, shipping, and I worked for the builders Wimpey, Laing and various other crews. I went mad. I stood outside the cafés, waiting for the vans to arrive and the gangers to select us if we were so blessed. All of this was too much for my delicate, artistic constitution. Once again, a musical instrument came my way, this time a mandolin, and this new addition led me to a life of busking in the underground. A real good life. I feel very proud that for a very brief time in my life I experienced the world of the Irish navvy, the construction worker. We had a book in secondary school called *Dialann Deoraí* (the diary of an Irish navvy), and I detested it. I don't know why it had such a toxic effect on me. It was a poor effort to describe the daily life of the Irish in exile. I felt it was a cruel, desperate view of the poor craytures who had to leave their homes for work and to make a living. When I met these people in Kilburn, Cricklewood and all over the ghettos, I felt I had met my own people, my own tribe. Being a 'townie' from back home made me a little different to most of them as I didn't come from a farming or rural background. What connected us was the music. I listened to, and learned, the music they knew and carried with them from home. The music, the culture, the language, the dance, the suffering and the sheer joy, these were our bond. I will never forget it, that world of the café, 'two slices ma'am', the site, the Mass, the Broadway, the bookie, the suit on Sunday, the smokes. I feel real privileged to have known the world of exile, the pilgrims on the lost highway, the tunnel tigers, the men and women who danced in The Galty, The Palais and The Gresham. Not to forget a lot of others who didn't fit into any community. These people were like me. There was John, Jimmy, Margaret, and a host of others I remember when I sing 'All Along the Watchtower' or 'Born in Mayo', or when I simply think of those times. A real good life.

Whenever I mention to some people that I busk on streets, or that my first professional music job, first real job, was busking, it immediately feels like they make a judgement about it, as if it's the same as begging, or maybe a little worse. The look in their eyes accuses, *wastin' your talent*. What they don't know is that for me, busking, playing music on the street or in the underground tube stations of London in the early '70s, was a truly wonderful experience on many levels. It was a full day's work. You had to 'book your pitch' hours in advance to get to play in the best venues. A lot of the buskers were seasoned pros, very independent, accomplished musicans who had great soul and integrity in their music-making. They inspired me no end. The music being played also suited my diverse and eclectic taste. Guitar pickers, people playing Bach and Vivaldi on mandolins and cellos, unaccompanied singers, West Indians singing and dancing, Irish musicians like me, playing and singing their own music from home. There were great cafés and pubs to meet up in and socialise with other buskers. One spot was the Kingsway Hall, a church run by a good man called Reverend Donald Soper. You could get dinner for a few pence. This place fed down-and-out people and all kinds of street dwellers. Homeless hobos like us, dining on the second floor of the church. Even this was a musical experience for us as the BBC orchestra practised their moves and their "beautiful art music" (as a man called it one day) in the hall below us. Imagine listening to André Previn conducting his orchestra while eating your shepherd's pie. Living underground in London was a very musical place to be in those days.

It sounded good to me to sing 'Hey Joe' or 'Boys of Barr na Sráide' in Oxford Circus tube station, and to play 'The March of the Kings of Laois' and 'O'Carolan's Concerto' at Marble Arch subway. One day a fella from home joined me on harp and we did our best to sound like Sonny Terry and Brownie McGee. I had heard these guys live in the 100 Club and it tore me up.

I found music everywhere I looked, even when I wasn't expecting it. I remember one November night I met a man called Darach Ó Cathain, he had no place to go and nowhere to stay, so I brought him back to where I was staying in Fulham. For to thank me, he sang the whole night, between talking and downing a brave few deoiríns (drops). I felt a very special presence that night with Darach singing 'Baile ui Lai' – a happy song of Raifteirí's, and 'An Beinnsín Luachra'. He was a very highly respected singer of the Conamara sean-nós tradition. He performed with Seán Ó Riada's Ceoltoirí Chualann when they first formed, and he also used to sing on the radio programme, *Reacaireacht an Riadaigh*. There is a CD of his singing called *Darach Ó Cathain*, it is one of the most special recordings of all. He died in 1987, but I hear Darach singing these songs still.

Fortunately, I just happened on the Irish Culture Club and this Irish music and in the White Hart Pub in Fulham, West London. I loved it, but it was alien to me. This was my first real connection with Irishness (especially the language, the sean-nós and the dance music), a connection I certainly did not have at home in Ireland. This is the irony of the exiled Irish. So, I studied it, devoured it, night and day, and listened and learned from the masters. It was full of passion and sweat, bacon and cabbage, rolled up smokes, gallons of light and bitter. A new language. I was getting my own story/history in sound. The true story from real people, outside of the official, clean version, the party line. I never believed history or school or anything.

I was learning, sometimes very quickly, all the things school avoided teaching us. As I listened to the best of music from Ireland, I felt sure that I was being taught about the life of the spirit through the language of music. It was all about music. The Favourite Pub on the Holloway Road was where I went to my Mass on Sunday mornings. These mornings were filled with poetry, songs (I used to be asked up for a song by Jimmy Power from Waterford), anarchists, republicans, communists, punks, construction workers, and their wives sometimes, misfits, con-men, con-women, dreamers, schemers and real decent folk. One May Sunday morning, I remember learning to play 'Lucy Campbell' and 'Toss the Feathers' from a busker outside this pub. He was a guitar player from Scotland with whom I will always associate these tunes.

I dashed off on my own to hear The Sex Pistols play with Siouxsie and the Banshees in the 100 Club, The Nashville Rooms and in Soho's El Paradiso. I stood in these places with the bands – The Bromley Crew and The Subway Sect. I witnessed the birthing process of punk aesthetics, which I recognised as really powerful and individual. 'Anarchy in the UK' and 'Pretty Vacant' were two songs at the time that said it all. I can never forget those sounds, those days and John Lydon, God bless him, sneering and singing. Brilliant. Bodies flying everywhere (like a few other times in my life!). I was never a real punk, nor was I ever a Paddy or a Mick either. I felt as if I fitted in nowhere. I wasn't one of the 'Johns' from North London who hung out on the Kings Road in McClaren's shop. I didn't support any particular football team, but I did support the Pistols, still do. John Lydon is a Galway man as far as I am concerned, 'Up Galway', The Tribesmen, our neighbours at home. There is an old saying in Ireland, *Mayo, God help us, Galway glad to have us*.

A lot of great punk and rock'n'roll music has come from the second-generation Irish in England. The Gallaghers, Morrissey (it sometimes seems that half of Manchester is Irish), Boy George, to name a few. The Pistols had it all (a bit like Wayne Rooney), power, art, songs, beauty and sheer terror of the present. These people were truly creative, and they reflected life as it was for them without all the trappings of privilege. They embodied it all, anger, truth, humour, and intelligence. I was a total fan.

Dylan, Nusrat Fatah, Cathal McConnell, The Sex Pistols, Alijah Bai Conti, John Doherty, all changed me forever, never to be the same again. As Dylan says, 'He who is not busy being born, is busy dying'.

The Troubadour coffee shop in Earl's Court was known as a famous folk club, except on Sundays when it turned into a Latin American 'free for all' session. I used to join in with my mandolin and I just *knew* the music: Cumbias from Colombia, Cuban tunes, Valse Criollos and 'winos' (Huaynos) from the Andes. I first heard of Victor Jara there. Many moons later, when visiting Lima and Cusco with my wife Isabela, I was reminded of the first time I heard the wonderful sound of this music. I loved it. Once again (like so many other times in my life), music acted as the signpost, this time pointing me in the direction of the Andes. I was glad to follow. I sang a few songs in Machu Picchu and saw some of the best dancing ever in Lima – Miraflores on Saturday night in the public park. Limeños (natives of Lima) dancing to old Cumbia music.

My own music-making was coming on in leaps and bounds. I was at it all day, every day. I got into the folk clubs as a floor singer, paying my way in as I never had any money (or 'bread' as the hippies said). I supported Martin Carty, Dave Swarbrigg, June Tabor, Ewan McColl and Peggy Seeger, and loads more. I also got recruited into some very rough, country and Irish bands. I remember well the rum and black outfits. 'Black Puddin'' and the 'Hills of Knocknashee' were some of the questionable musical offerings of that time. I got on fine with the other band members who saw me as a bit of a character, a bit daft. They were all fine, straight, upstanding Irishmen. They took no drink and didn't smoke, sensible lads. I am very grateful to all the bands and people I met along the way. It was all good for learning, playing in the Irish pubs was sort of sad at times, but it was also great entertainment.

Needless to say, I moved away from country and Irish music and the Galty and The Gresham ballrooms. I was a 'townie', a 'fish-head' (slang for a Castlebar native) and a biteen odd, different, always on the move. I was listening a lot to Django Reinhardt, *Blonde on Blonde* by Dylan, and *Paddy in the Smoke*. My taste in music at this stage also included reggae and ska. My party pieces were 'The Deportees' and Chuck Berry's 'C'est la Vie...the Teenage Wedding.' God help us. We had a small, but loyal, following (unemployed generally) in the pubs, clubs and traps of North London.

Early on, after my arrival in London town, I tried a few employment agencies looking for 'the start'. I think my first posting was to a warehouse near Brixton tube station, working with a loyal band of Jamaican lads, packing mannequins for export to the fashion houses of the world. It was a howl. I was the only Paddy (as I was known) present. All day long reggae – fantastic music that I love to this day. Toots and the Maytals, The Heptones, Desmond Dekker, Jimmy Cliff, Ska – The Skatelites (Don Drummond was a music hero of mine), Marcia Griffiths' 'Survival', The Paragons' 'Feed the Fire, Fan the Flame', 'We the People Who Are Darker than Blue' and on and on. Of course the air was filled with ganja, and there was lots of dancing too – I think. A week or two I lasted until I rode off, me and Clint Eastwood, into the sunset. Nevertheless, this particular job greatly boosted my love of Jamaican music and culture.

Around the same time, I saw the movie *The Harder They Come* with Jimmy Cliff playing the part of the outlaw Ivan O'Martin in Perry Henzell's film. This film to me is timeless – a story of a young man's move from the country to the city and all the trauma that comes with it. I totally appreciated the sheer raw beauty of the soundtrack which Perry said was "The best week's work I ever did!" It is incredible that it took less than a week to put the music together for this film. I felt then, but not so much now, the song 'Living Here in Limbo' best described my days and nights in London. 'Sure as the sun will shine, I'm gonna get my share now, what's mine...'

I lived sometimes around Notting Hill. I used to busk on Portobello Road of a Saturday, and maybe do a gig or play a session of Irish music in the Elgin Pub in Ladbroke Grove. I loved the vibe, the music, 'the colours man' around this part of London. Van Morrison's presence was all around, 'Saw you walking, down by Ladbroke Grove this morning, with your brand new boy and your Cadillac', 'Astral Weeks', 'TB sheets' and 'Them and Us'.

My soul was always filled with music and song as my life seemed to flicker by like a slide show. No future, no ambition, nothing mattered except the next one, the next 'hit', the next jug of ale. I was selfish and self-centred, but I believe today that I was saved by music and '...the song she was hummin'. Glory O, glory O, to the bold Fenian men'.

Our lives in London (the rovers, nomads, exiles, navvies) didn't seem to matter to anyone else, at home or abroad. We were reacting to the hand we were dealt in life. All in the same boat, just about keeping afloat, '...merrily, life is but a dream...'

I learned Irish music and the Irish language in London, from people who had it from birth. I loved it. I loved being away with the fairies, being an immigrant, a stranger, a drunk. I couldn't imagine living any other sort of life as I wondered around the great city of London, heartbroken, homeless, blessed, loving it and hating it, humming and strumming 'The Banks Hornpipe' and squattin' in Kilburn in a mansion with the boys from the County Mayo. Most of them gone on today, Slí na Fírinne (the way of the truth).

So boys pull together,
in all kinds of weather.
Don't show the white feather
wherever ye go.
Be as a brother,
help one another,
like true hearted men
from the County Mayo.
(Traditional)

'While we honour in song and in story...', I don't think a day passes without me singing or playing a tune in honour of these good people who helped, guided and befriended this poor soul as I sang and danced my songline in those heady, intense, and dangerous times. God bless you all, you are in the music forever, 'In the smoke' mar a déarfá (as they say).

Swift the Thames flows to the sea,
bearing ships and part of me.
('Sweet Thames', Ewan McColl)

THE WHITE FEATHER

(John Hoban)

I've seen lots of men and some women,
as I ramble from shore to shore.
I've friends in many states of mind
who allow me stop on the floor.
I'm now in my fortieth year
of singing and dancing my way.
Please God, I'll live till I'm eighty,
I'll have twice as much to say.

I keep seeing new people and places
I'm in California today.
Singing in San Francisco
looking out on its beautiful bay.
I feel so blessed in this lifetime,
to be given a chance to forgive,
myself for being such a pagan,
and not having a clue how to live.

So, boys get together don't speak of weather,
leave the turf and the hay,
to the neighbours at home,
heal one another,
let go of your mother,
be glad that you come from
the County Leitrim!

Notes on the song:

From a very young age, we were taught never to show the 'white feather' – never to show who you really are, don't let anyone know you, keep it all under wraps. I believe this was so wrong. It was a code which commanded us to always look well, sound well, and let no one get close enough to see how fragile and vulnerable we really are. So, this song is a step in the other direction, as I try each day of my life to do the opposite to what I was taught. Each day I try to let somebody know who I am, and I also try to listen and to help them be themselves. Music and singing are the best ways I have found to do this.

BORN IN MAYO

(John Hoban)

We were born in Mayo forty years ago,
the biggest job, right now, is letting go.
The past, the future, what'll the neighbours say.
Those chains that stopped us living for today.

We were born in Mayo forty years ago,
at sixteen from there we were forced to go.
We took the boat to Holyhead, lived in fear, right on the edge.
Digging drains in London in the snow.

Tried to figure out how a boy became a man.
Sleeping rough in the West End in a red van.
Nobody could tell me what I was all about,
so in a few short days, I was back where I began.

Hung out with the rebels, loners, tramps.
Singing on streets, moving with Travellers' camps.
My best friend turned on me, plainly I could see
the game was over, the crowds were heading home.

Looked for help then I heard the truth.
One man's story felt the same as mine.
I learned to listen, learned to share.
To do the best I could do.
I forgave myself and then again I met you.

We were born in Mayo forty years ago.
The biggest job, right now, is letting go.
The past, the future, what'll the neighbours say.
Those chains that stopped
us living for today.

Notes on the song:

The story is about two people initially going their separate ways but by the end of the song, they join forces to walk together on the pathway to freedom and new happiness.

Chapter 7

IRELAND, MOTHER IRELAND

With my fiddle and banjo,
I've covered some ground,
from Belfast to Boston,
and dear Achill Sound.
Okemah, Oklahoma to old Santa Fe,
the place I call home,
is 'round the shores of Clew Bay.
('Knight of the Road', John Hoban)

L ondon, with all the rich, diverse, colourful, vibrant songs, the talk and the tunes led me back to visit the four corners of my native land. It led me to seek out the music, the masters, the source, and the hidden glorious world of the spirit. Somehow, the mystery of it all put me in mind of the smokes the patients begged from us kids when we visited 'The Mental' in Castlebar. I just kept moving from pillar to post, from townland to village to city, seeking the old music. Thatched houses, canvas tents, teepees, hippies, benders, alternative this and that, normal folks, but mostly dark, dusty corners where we dropped anchor and congregated in song, dance, music and madness.

This went on and on, and almost to the tragic end for me. It did end tragically for quite a few of my friends. Alcohol and its allies were a constant, even sometimes referred to as 'the cure'. Some cure. Music again was vital. It soothed my soul and gave me strength. It saved my life on many occasions.

At this stage, I was hanging on for dear life and on a constant diet of music. I was playing the banjo and bouzouki, singing and moving from town to town. But equally important, I was listening to every sort of music that came my way. I'd be staying in different houses (sometimes different counties) every second night depending on where the music would move me to. I would always be listening to other people's LPs or record collections.

75

I loved exploring music I'd never heard before. For example, in 1972-73 I was very much into Bob Dylan's *Blood on the Tracks*, Andy McGann's music (the great Irish fiddler in New York), J.S. Bach's Cello Suites, any flamenco or Cajun music I could hear, John Coltrane, Sandy Denny singing anything, but especially 'Who Knows Where the Time Goes?', and more.

In the early 1970s, I met up with Connie Cullen and Red Quigly in the Asgard pub in Westport. They were from Dundalk. They were good singers, and good people. Some friends of theirs also drifted over to the West where it was said 'the livin' is easy, fish are jumpin' and the cotton is high'. Next I was down in Ennis, County Clare, busking, listening and learning, when I met Eilis O'Connor and her brothers Gerry and Peter, fiddle players of high renown, also from the town of Dundalk. We got on famously. I also befriended Leon Agnew, the flute player, in Gurteen, County Sligo at a Michael Coleman commemoration weekend. Leon lived in, and played music around Dundalk. So, it seemed inevitable that I would go to visit Dundalk, to check it out, with a one way ticket. I think this was in 1979 – years didn't register very clearly with me during these hazy days. I felt like a cork on the ocean, like a feather in the wind as I tramped all over the country following the ceol (music). It was leading me by the hand.

Early on in my sojourn in County Louth, I was busking outside the post office on Clanbrassil Street, Dundalk. Two fine men invited me for a cup of tea and a chat, so off I go with them to the Fane Bar. They inquired if I would be willing to teach music out in the Cooley Penninsula. "Yes," said I, "I would," but I had to check with my 'manager' first (whoever my manager might be seeing as I only had a banjo, the clothes I was wearing and not a penny to my name!). I always knew I could rely on music and on my ability to teach. I was hired.

For a few days each week for a year or so, I hitched out to the Cooley Kickhams' Hall and to Carlingford where I taught a lot of children the music which I had myself been given. I would head back into Dundalk for the evening, have a feed in Brady's Café, or in some other kind household, of which there were many. From then on, I'd play for the rest of the day in Peter McManus's bar, Mark McLoughlin's bar, Jimmy and Maureen Kennedy's in Stabannon, and any other houses, sheebeens, or sheds that would have me. I learned to sing and play a lot of music in these days. I recall meeting Tommy McArdle in Stabannon one time. Tommy was the brother of Peter, a wonderful fiddle player who had passed away by the time I reached Mark's bar (although I think I meet him sometimes in the spirit world). Peter greatly influenced the O'Connors, Oliver Tennyson and Imor Byrne, the musicians from whom I had learned the tunes, 'The Day the Ass Ran Away' and 'Tickle Her Leg with a Barley Straw' and many more. The music goes around in circles and I was learning Dundalk music in Dublin, and in the town itself. I loved 'the town' as it was known, and I think of it as being an especially honest and creative place.

My time spent in Castle Lane, Castlebar, in Christy Hoban's house of high renown, best of bacon, stood me in good stead as I helped my friend J.J. with his new venture of selling fruit and veg. This job helped me to supplement the 'coupons' (local term for money). We sold fruit and veg all around the town of Dundalk. J.J. used to sing while I rolled the smokes. I remember 'The Piano Man' was all the go, a big hit for both Billy Joel and, I believe, for J.J. in Germany when he was over there working. I'd give my best to 'Poncho and Lefty' and 'Exodus, Movement of Jah People'. We sold only the best fruit and veg and I learned that even the poor cabbage had a heart! I felt totally at home selling fruit and veg around Fatima, St Nicholas Avenue, Muirhevnamor, and all over the streets and housing estates of Dundalk. When I was there around Christmas time, I was invited to more houses for the dinner, music and chat than I ever was anywhere else. There was an amazing heart to Dundalk people, and I felt more at home there than I did anywhere else I had been. Musically, it was very powerful for me.

Being a border town, Dundalk was full of music and people from the Northern counties and towns. I always felt a great closeness to these Northern people and I loved the music from these places. Dundalk was a very important place for me, it gave me a great chance to learn music and to play with all kinds of musicans and singers. I used to go to the North for gigs, sessions, and fleadh cheoils (festivals of music) all the time. I felt protected by the music, and I never had a day's bother in Belfast, Down, Armagh or anywhere else. My friend Leon, the flute player, was a true friend and teacher to me in those days. Fair play.

Music taught me that every place has its unique sound or accent, Ardboe, Ardglass, Keenagh, Derry, Claregalway. Everywhere.

Sligo too was special because the music has lived on there, within the people, for eons. The picture is somewhat different in County Mayo, especially in West Mayo, where musicians seem to have taken the boat into exile or, in many cases, went underground. Sligo, of course, had Coleman, Killoran, Morrison and flute players galore. I recall one beautiful sunny day when I was busking in O'Connell Street (in the centre of Sligo), a man, whom I had never met before, just walked up to me, took out a concert flute, asked me if I knew 'The Knotted Chord', and then proceeded to play this beautiful music. His name was Pakie Duignan. He also played some of John McKenna's reels. He had a fine suit on him with his winner's medal from the fleadh cheoil in the jacket lapel. Wonderful. How could I go wrong?

I had no formal music education at all. In fact, I did not feel I had a tradition. I was not sure about what people referred to as 'styles of music' or 'settings of tunes'. I did, however, recognise how different individuals played and presented the music. Each county in Ireland held for me a treasure of sound, each county unique. I was totally drawn in by the colours and rythms expressed by the great people I encountered musically. I feel, as each day passes, more grateful than I can ever express by the way musicians (too numerous to mention) gave me their time and patience. It seems to me the music must be passed on freely and with respect in order to grow. I can remember almost the exact time and place I received a particular song or tune. I can also recall exactly how I was *travellin'* at the time, what the score was, the craic. This is a true way of remembering and respecting those times, and those people who passed on the music to me. It is also a way of honouring my own journey, past, present and future.

The same idea applies to some contemporary music I have heard and learned from recordings, or by chance meetings. For example, I went to a concert to hear a wee man by the name of Alijah Bai Conti in Trinity College in 1987. He played the Kora, a lute harp from the Gambia in West Africa. He sang and played for two hours to eleven people, including myself. Nobody had heard of him I suppose, or else they were busy elsewhere. I felt so moved, I cried and laughed. I went up to him afterwards and asked him how did he learn music (I always ask that question of people as I feel it is the primary question). He replied to me in broken English, "My grandfather and seven more grandfathers!" I met his son, Denbo Conti, in Galway two years later and asked him how I could buy a Kora. He graciously sold me the one he was playing, so now I play it for myself at home. He made the instrument himself, and I feel honoured to have the Kora and to be making my own sound on it, strange harp-like music, in County Mayo. All the way from the Gambia. The Conti people are what are known as Griots or Bards. Like the old bards in Ireland, way before my time chronologically, but extremely close to me spiritually. I felt a very strong connection to these people, their lives and their music.

One day in Dublin, while busking, my good friend Desi Wilkinson came along and introduced me to Cathal McConnell. The three of us then played together on Mary Street, two flutes and a banjo. We played a request of 'Danny Boy' for a poor man on the wine, who looked like he might not see another day. It made his day, and mine. We made no money, but it sure was a great event, a great learning in life, in music and in the service of playing music for others – the giving of our gift for the good of others. Cathal McConnell is one of my first real heroes, a true teacher in Irish traditional music. He comes from Fermanagh, and was playing with a world-famous outfit called The Boys of the Lough. I had seen him in concert in The Eagle Tavern in New York. Now here he was with Desi Wilkinson and yours truly, playing on Mary Street for anybody and everybody – even the gardaí – free of charge and for fun. A great man, a great musician/singer, and to me, a great teacher, and a great example of a true artist. Desi, in my books, is one of the best I've ever met. A great musician, singer, and gentleman.

Another great musical experience came my way on a bright September morning in Donegal, 1971. As myself and my mate Bernard were trying to hitch a lift out of Glenties, a man crossed over the road to talk to us when he heard me playing a tune on the mandolin. He directed us to a wee pub, an 'early house', O'Faolain's I think was the name over the door. Inside, the great man himself, John Doherty, was visiting for the day.

Hear the voice of the Bard!
Who Present, Past and Future sees
Whose ears have heard,
The Holy Word,
That walk'd among the ancient trees.
('Songs of Experience', William Blake)

We, Bernard and I (the visitors), were put sitting beside John himself. We had no money, but we were given food and drink all day as we sat in awe and wonder at what was going on. John Doherty spoke, sang, danced and played the fiddle until six o'clock that evening. He gave the greatest performance – if you can call it so – of Irish music I have ever experienced. Even now I get the most powerful, warm, inspirational feelings when I think back on that day. He introduced each piece of music with a wonderful story, moving between the Irish and the English languages. He asked me if I would play for him on the mandolin. I gave my best and I also sang a song. I remember thinking, *What will I play for this man at all?* My best had to come out. I didn't have many tunes or songs, so I played the 'Foxhunter's Reel'. I know that I played my best but I'm sure it was a pretty innocent rendition of the tune. John Doherty praised my music, and made sure the 'audience' showed appreciation too. He then said to me, very quietly and kindly, "I'll play the same tune for you the way I got it." He announced to the listeners that he would play a piece of music on the fiddle that was composed before people could write music. It was called 'The Hare and the Hound'. My God. Talk about being blown away. I was moved to tears and till the day I die, I will never forget his descriptive fox chase piece. It still rings in my soul and in my heart. Afterwards, he asked if I would sing a song, so I sang 'The Faithful Sailor Boy' which I heard first from The Keanes of Carlestrane in County Galway. He listened with his eyes closed, thanked me again, and gave me such wonderful support and encouragement for my efforts at music. I felt blessed beyond words. Maybe six people were present all day, and in the evening, his great friend, the doctor, called for him and away he went.

I have since learned that both John Doherty and his brother Mickey are buried in Fintown Cemetery in County Donegal. A friend of mine visited the grave and he told me that it's easy to find. Growing out of it is a mountain ash tree, a beautiful, humble tree which bears berries each year to feed the blackbirds. The day I met John Doherty in Glenties he spoke so lovingly of the blackbird, and of course he played the air, the set dance and the reel called 'The Blackbird' (which I once saw my mother dance) in an extraordinary fashion.

My rambles also took me to the South of Ireland on many occasions where I met singers on the street like Geordie Hanna from County Tyrone, and Nicholas Toibin from County Waterford. I had heard of both these men before and I loved their singing. They opened up to me immediately and sang song after song, as if we were lifelong friends, as if they knew that music was our first language, as if it was more natural to sing than to rattle on talking about the weather. 'Old Ardboe', 'Lisburn Town', 'Na Conneries' (in whose house I was later to lodge in Camperdown, Sydney, Australia), 'An Caisideach Bán', were all passed on to me on the streets of Thurles and Listowel. I was feeling increasingly more like a musician as I learned from all the people I was meeting on my path.

Another ramble brought me to AnCo training centre in Galway to learn welding. I lasted three days maybe, then on my last day, I walked out and just kept walking until I reached Mrs. Cullen's in Foster Street. There was a session of music and drink in full swing in the bar, middle of the day. I never welded again.

While busking (down on my luck, hungry, thirsty, confused) in Waterford city one day, 'the Pecker', Padraic Dunne, stopped and gave me encouragement and showed me kindness. I will always remember these times, singing and playing to live. Just to live. During times like this I felt that I didn't have anything else to do or to live for. All of these encounters were, and are, hugely important in my life. In fact, I feel that these chance meetings with the 'music people' saved my life. I only had music, nothing else. It was my entire life. I didn't have a past, and I certainly had no future. I didn't have a home, a country, a job or career. All I had was the song they were singing and the grace and gift of music I was receiving. These people weren't only my heroes, they were masters of music, song and sound. They stood and sang for me because I believe that some energy, or higher power, directed it to happen. I have had many other experiences and musical/spiritual events in my life.

It was a long and a windy road that brought me here. It was a good road that tended to me. A hard and a hungry road as many of my kind fell by the wayside. I think of them today as I listen and ramble and sing. I connect with these spirits always, a communion of souls. I sing and play for them with humility and respect. They passed all this music and the stories on to me so that I may pass them on and carry the tradition on. Buíochas le Dia (thanks be to God).

KNIGHT OF THE ROAD
– FIDDLE AND BANJO

(John Hoban)

I'm a ramblin' man from the County Mayo
When spring comes around
I'm willin' to go,
wherever my spirit longs to be.
The road is my friend,
it takes care of me.

(Chorus)
With my fiddle and banjo
I've covered some ground.
From Belfast to Boston
and dear Achill Sound.
Okemah, Oklahoma, and old Santa Fe.
But the place I call home
is 'round the shores of Clew Bay.

I met two black swans, in Queensland one day,
they restored me to sanity,
like making hay.
I spent three days by train,
crossed the Nullarbor Plain,
with no tree in sight,
nearly went insane.

It was great to arrive in New Mexico,
to be met off the bus by a man from Mayo.
We played music with cowboys and Indians too.
We 'saddled the pony' for the Navajo and Sioux.

Istanbul is in a world of its own,
met a father and son play a fiddle and drum,
in a shop that was close
to a thousand years old.
We sang and we danced,
till the cats came home.

While I'm still young at heart,
I'll ramble I'll say,
playing this music,
for an honest day's pay.
When he calls me ashore,
I'll be ready to go,
far from the blue hills
of County Mayo.

Notes on the song:
This song came down from Curraun Hill, Achill, County
Mayo, one day in spring. It sets off on the road to New Mexico,
the dustbowl of Oklahoma and back again with the wind to the
shores of Clew Bay. Then away to Turkey, Australia, the Nullarbor Plain, the plain of no trees, and back again to Clew Bay.

CRAZY HORSE

(John Hoban)

In the middle of the country
behind Croagh Patrick
in a wee thatched house
that's now in poor repair
lived this quiet little music man,
not many knew him.
Put me in mind of Crazy Horse
with his feathers and white hair.

Any day and us coming home,
from school daydreaming,
you'd be sure to pick up
on strange sounds you'd likely hear.

The silence carries clearly
the flute or lonesome singing,
it sort of cast a spell on us,
as we stood in the crossroads.

Many moons later,
us squattin' 'beyant' in Kilburn,
we came across the same vibe,
in a pub in Cricklewood.
We bid farewell to the subbies,
to the diggin' and the dossin'.
Farewell to McAlpine,
we were rockin' from here on out.

The sounds that we followed were unique,
like Skip James.
Like the clash of the ash,
like the howlin' of the wolf.
The sounds were very beautiful,
like the playing of Coleman,
like the sound of the skylark,
soar high but for his grace.

So, we tramped and we traipsed,
to the corners of Ireland,
from Wexford to Belfast,
from Dublin to Mayo.
We searched every townland,
every village, every valley,
to meet up with these people,
we knew only by their sound.

Some of them played boxes,
others stroked fiddles,
some were raw singers,
while others made strong tae,
some of them danced stories,
others studied '25'.
But all of them knew heartache,
by the number all their lives.

Most of them have passed on
to meet up with their Maker,
who knows what follows after,
or what awaits for them on high?
I'm so, so glad I heard them singing,
saw them dance and disappearing,
back into the land or sea,
or from which they came.

Notes on the song:
A story about following the sound of music. A story about the type of people I followed. A story about trusting what is up ahead because of the goodness and truth that comes out in the sound and the energy of music stories. For me, faith in a higher power is the beginning and end of it all. So, that's what Crazy Horse is kinda about. Not easy to follow. Simple but not easy. I once heard Sufi musicianers say, 'freedom is the absence of choice'. Too true, Horse.

Chapter 8

THE TRADITIONAL...

He was humming an old jig that I'd never heard,
it sounded so lonesome, so high and so clear.
He drained the last drop. He bid me adieu,
and the song that I've sung, has the same tune for you.
('A Day out in Sligo', John Hoban)

When I returned to the 'hood (Castlebar, Mayo) in the '70s, the traditional music was beginning to catch on like a new fashion. There was a folk club in the Imperial Hotel, which brought in people like Fred Finn and Peter Horan as guests. Kenny's pub on Main Street (now a thriving Chinese restaurant) hosted the first sessions of ceol in the town, The Live Show. A few musicians kept it going, people like Mick Monaghan, and before him Martin Ruane and Snooky Ellwood, who was a street banjo player. A short time later, a few of us got together in the Humbert Inn, also on Main Street, and started a band called General Humbert. When we got our act together, I decided to leave and travel the roads to discover more music. The band became quite famous without me, fair play to them! At this time in Ireland, many bands were beginning to appear on the scene. I saw Planxty myself when they first started, as support to Donovan Leitch:

First there is a mountain, then there is no mountain,
then there is...

I liked to go and hear Planxty play as I was fond of their blend of songs and traditional music especially on the pipes. I have always loved Christy's way, even more so these times. His music with Declan Sinnott gets deeper and more powerful by the day. As Dylan said in New York in 1968, "I am a firm believer in the longer you live, the better you get." I understand where Christy and Declan are coming from musically and thankfully, providence saw that our paths crossed not only on 'Paddy's Green Shamrock Shore' but also on Van Diemen's Land. It is all about music and friendship. I have learned oceans about songs and life from my friend Christy. Hopefully, I give back as good as I can. Fad saol (long life), as they say in Achill.,

Planxty, with the talents of Dónal and Andy, were a refreshing, exciting musical sound in my life in those days. I especially followed Sweeney's Men, as I wrote earlier. Johnny Moynihan would be a very valuable influence on my own singing and playing to this day. He was the man who introduced the bouzouki into Irish music. I think Johnny is a real important innovator in music and an original musical voice.

The Chieftains and De Danann were on the go in the early '70s too, I suppose everyone was thinking about making a few bob out of the traditional in those days. Why not? Go for it lads. At last, an interest in traditional Irish music.

The Humbert Inn had music sessions going continuously. The sessions were open and free to the public. We were all full of ourselves and full of porter, all the time. This was all new to Castlebar life, and we were discovering ourselves in so many ways. The music was like a back-drop to our lives. The Humbert days inspired younger lads and lassies to take up the traditional and to try to make music.

I never felt comfortable in any band situation, even though I was to play in quite a few such as Muigh Eo, Arcady, Bumblebees, Big City, and céilí bands. I simply didn't enjoy the experience. I did not feel true to either myself, or to the music. Giving songs and tunes back to an audience in the form of learned repertoire seemed to lack spontaneity and individual expression. It lacked soul. It reminded me of school exams, so it had to go. I understand and respect others' desire to perform in bands, but it is not for me. I feel music should flow freely from a place in the heart that can not be dictated to by any outer authority. Peace and Love, man. Let music flow like a river, natural like.

Feeling good was good enough for me,
good enough for me and Bobby McGee.
('Me and Bobby McGee', Kris Kristofferson)

During this same period, I was first asked to teach music to children. I knew I could sing and compose lots of songs, all types of songs. I could play fiddle, banjo, kora, accordian, guitar, mandolin, bouzouki, harmonica, bodhrán, and many more instruments. However, teaching is a totally different gift compared to playing and performing. I soon discovered that I had this gift for passing the music on. I could do this, and do it well.

Here is an excerpt from an interview done by Heather Marshall about my teaching, songwriting and creativity:

An active musician, songwriter and teacher, John Hoban is a well-known figure in the Mayo area. Interested in everything from local archaeology, geography and social history he travels internationally, both teaching and performing music. Sees himself as an instrument/channel of communication for conveying the language of music. Determinedly non-materialistic and advocating the pursuit of a simple life, he resembles (and may just well be) one of the very last travelling bards.

John Hoban's technique is to listen to his inner self, his inner voice. Asked if the words are written first or the tune he replied, "If words come from the heart the music and rhythm are in the words – it is all one thing." He is not concerned with quantity of production driven by commercial demands but rather with quality. Love versus fear emerge as spur and impediment respectively to his creativity. Factors which block the creative process are fear, the self, the ego. These have to be acknowleged and discarded to create space to live and engage creatively. Establishing a dialogue through listening and response in an unconditional way is like loving or giving and fosters creative output. He looks beneath the surface and tries to capture the qualities of simplicity and truth in subjects which he finds in the global landscape and the people around him. Writing songs is living, walking, breathing. It is not a question of 'how many songs did you produce this year?' but that every encounter is a song. Children characteristsically sing their story, Aborigines walk their songlines – we are all born with equal music.

John's musical technique has developed primarily by 'doing' and this is the message in his teaching. He has been playing music for the last 40 years. Prior to that he has listened to music and has been singing and dancing since the day he was born. Among his teachers have been all those who have played music with him from every imaginable background. He describes them as still with him metaphorically speaking as a circle of saints, always at his shoulder. In John's class academic musical theory is not given so much emphasis as simply getting on and doing it. When he plays with other musicians there is no formal rehearsal; the performance is spontaneous with improvisation fitting the mood and moment.

His many teachers have each in their way inspired him. He acknowledges learning from others who gave him the permission to be himself musically and therefore to learn and develop. His greatest inspiration is silence. Meditation is important. Being awake, living a life that is worthwhile, looking beyond the surface for the underlying truth, sensing the rhythm of words, being aware of feelings all contribute to inspire.

He lives a simple life – not necessarily an easy one. Unencumbered by distractions and unnecessary possessions he lives for the moment – for the 'now'. A varied network of 'musical friends' from 'Belfast to Boston' ('Fiddle and Banjo'), New York, Ontario and Sydney interact with John and engage in a lively musical dialogue of ideas, songs and tunes. The creative process is not over laboured but occurs typically naturally, almost inevitably – like breathing, through contem-

plation of tranquil surroundings of favourite haunts in Achill
or episodes of his own life's journey.

The story of his own life and influences, his travels and trials provide abundant original souce of material for his songs.
Certainly the 'knights of the road' drinking tea in his mother's
kitchen years ago passed John Hoban a creative spark or two
from the fireside.

I have taught music to many, many people of all ages. I am
still teaching. I love it, the method, the individual expression.
From day one, the development of my life in music was always
going to lead me to teaching and passing on my songs and tunes
in West Mayo. For me, it was a natural progression, part of my
journey. I was also seeking out musicians in every corner of the
County Mayo. Some were to be found in the psychiatric hospital, St. Mary's, where I visited regularly. One resident told me
his story. He told me that he was put away in the '60s by his kin
for playing the tin whistle and talking to the birds. He was a
wonderful person, and I learned music from him. 'Off to California' and the 'Three Little Drummers' were from Richard.
He's always around, like a robin.

Traditional music was not at all popular where I came from,
and neither was folk music. There was little to no traditional
music being played in Westport and Castlebar and their sur-
rounding areas during the 1970s. Pubs only started to have music when the tourist asked for it, or so it seemed to me. A lot
of players had switched over in the '60s to play modern popular music, leaving the traditional behind. Showbands, singing
lounges, fancy footwork and velvet suits were all the rage. So,
when I started teaching traditional music to children in Mayo,
I was aware that the wider community wasn't too familiar with
slides, or the Tulla Céilí Band, or with traditional music in general. Sean-nós singing and dancing were even more unfamiliar
to them.

I trawled the country for music and for musicians from whom
I could learn, and with whom I could play. This was a strange

experience to me. I was so glad to have met Tom Needham, Joe Keane, Billy Gallagher, the Stauntons in Tourmakeady and the Mayocks from Ross (I have fond memories of great Sunday nights in Paddy Hoban's on Main Street playing with this young family, it was the highlight of my week). There were more, Julie Langan, the Kilroys, and Rosaleen Stenson Ward, and a few other families who were great lovers of, and later, great players of the traditional. Walter Sammon was a great friend of mine at this time too.

I remember hitching down Quay Hill in Westport one dark November night in the '70s to join up with the Staunton family for a bit of music. I met up with Pat, Mary, Kathleen and Catherine-Anne in the Asgard Tavern. I had a bouzouki, or a banjo, and little else with me. The Stauntons were a real joy for me, a musical oasis. They were very young at the time but they played really lovely music. Both parents and grandparents had music, as they say.

My good friend Walter also had music from both sides of his family. He played the bodhrán, the bones (human ones!), and later the box. 'He was ploughing the raging main', or, in another words, he worked as an engineer at sea with Irish Shipping, travelling the Seven Seas. His time on *terra firma* was spent between his home, and travelling away all over the country, following and seeking out the traditional, the ceol, the music. This man gave me a present of a fiddle, from Liverpool, which I value, cherish, and play to this day, everyday. Thanks again, a chara (my friend).

I think a music tradition takes a long time to build up. Thousands of years maybe. James O'Malley, or James Gulf, as he was known, was a tin whistle player whom I loved to listen to. I learned a lot about music and life from James. A noble, gentle man, a true friend in music and a true friend to me. So too was Jack Harte and his great neighbour, Tom Heneghan, Francie Mack, Rose Nixon, Dominic Grady, John Chambers, Paddy Kilroy and Mick Barrett, real music people. These people kept the tradition going in small pockets throughout Mayo. They did this for the love of it. This is the music that fed my soul and, as each day passes, I become ever more grateful for the gift of music.

In the '60s, the only music I heard coming from the Royal Ballroom was imitations of American country music, and imitations of pop music from the USA and England. Everybody wanted to be somebody else. They sounded like they came from Texas or Nashville, not from Kiltimagh or County Monaghan or Tucker Street in Castlebar. It was as if they had disassociated themselves from where they came from. Some things never change. The people followed the crowd, living life by numbers. It never appealed to me.

The genuine music people I met were almost all rebels, loners, individuals of a sort, who had a very small, but dedicated band of artistic and genuine followers. For example, often, my good friend and music man, Norman, and I used to make our way to Jack Halpin's Ale House in Ballyhaunis on a Monday night. I knew that Mary Staunton, from Tourmakeady, played and sang there, and she was joined by a host of wonderful people who played, sang and listened to music of the highest quality: Mick Conroy, Dominic and Mary Rush, Jimmy Killeen, John Austin Freehily, Andy Flanagan, the Waldrons and sometimes Dermot Grogan, to name a few. Almost all gone to their Maker now, but I have kept the music I learned from them and continuously pass it on to all those I teach, my students, or anyone that happens to come along. The likes of those evenings were not big, loud affairs. In fact, Jack almost vetted his customers as to their eligibility to attend these sacred sessions. It was like a crowd of Native Americans, wise men and women, sharing the medicine in the sweat lodge.

These times seem to be just a wonderful memory now. However, when I play the 'Broken Pledge', 'Miss Monaghan', or 'Wallop the Spot', I hear a 'B' flat set of uileann pipes, or I hear the tin whistle style of that area and of that era. These memories bring to mind a line in 'Danny Boy', 'I will live in peace until you come to me'.

My teaching has brought me to Achill, Westport, Clare Island, and all places in between. Not too many of those I taught continue to play music. Many were forced into lessons, competitions and performances for the sake of their parents, the school or for Mother Ireland. As soon as they could drop the music, they did. And then they took to the hills.

It is my belief that competition, and cravings for fame and financial gain, kill the soul of music. My experience has taught me that traditional music should not be read from a sheet of paper, but *ó ghluain go gluin*, from knee to knee. I fully appreciate the value in being able to read music, however, it is my opinion that this method of learning destroys the music from the soul. A fiddle and a violin may be the same instrument, but how they are played are worlds apart. A lot of older musicians had the ability to read music, were musically literate, however, they chose to learn by listening to others. Traditional music is an oral tradition passed down through generations, learned by ear. No traditional musician plays music with a book in front of them, or a book in their head (unlike a classical musician whose reference is the printed text).

The question 'Did you learn by note or did you learn by ear?' has been put to me many times, hundreds of times probably. Another question that is shot at me as often has been 'What kind of music do you play?' I will try to address both questions honestly and briefly. The answer to the first one is that everything I've learned has been by eighty per cent listening and twenty per cent practice (roughly). I picked up from the older musicians that the only way to learn and to play music is by ear, as it is called. I feel if a person learns by note or solely from reading music notation, they have closed down the greatest of all musical attributes, which is the ability to play and to listen at the same time. It is not possible to play with others without this talent or gift. All a person becomes is a voice that must be followed, that must dominate other voices, or else a person must become like a worker on a musical assembly line playing only the one part as instructed. It is what happens in orchestras, rock bands, céilí bands, all bands in fact. Some people love that role. I never took to it myself even though I read music fairly well, just like most of the older masters from whom I learned music. They too read notes in books but chose to learn by ear for a few reasons:

🌸 It was the way the music, all music, was passed on for generations throughout the world.

🌸 It meant people could listen to each others' individual expression of music and learn from each other.

🌸 People remembered the music far better when learned by ear. It seems to come from the heart rather than the head.

Music books, and collections of songs and music play a very important role in preserving the music as an archival resouce – a wonderful resource. They continue to be of great value today.

As for the question about what sort of music I play, I always answer by saying that I play my own brand of music. A mixture of all kinds. No category. No label. No Rules. Just from the heart. It's not the answer that is looked for usually. Ná bac leis (not to worry).

In teaching, I try my best to pass it on as I got it. I am still working with this method. It is an individual approach to music rather than the group or *one size fits all* approach. It comes from the heart, to the heart. My experience has led me to totally oppose all competition in music. Who can say one person is better at singing than another? Competition, like stardom and status in music or art, instills a fear within us which stops us expressing ourselves in the wonderful world of music, which is God-given in us all. I encourage always, – Mol *an óige agus tiocfaidh siad* (Irish proverb-praise the young and they will respond) – and I teach never to compare ourselves to others, and never to judge others. I also encourage people to keep an open mind in music, and to listen closely and learn from all kinds of music, from the Gambia to Peru, from Donegal to Dun Chaoin, from Mozart to Mali from Howlin' Wolf to Margaret Barry, then, ar aghaidh linn (on with us).

Around this time in the '70s, people were discovering that there was plenty of money – *beaucoup de* bucks – to be made from the music. With money-making in the picture, it all changed. The music was owned and run by a false market of non-artists, business heads, organisations, and much ego-driven self-promotion. A far cry from the hob-nailed boot crew 'deep in the heart of London town', or the turned-down wellingtons dancing sets in Clare Island. I said good luck to them, one and all. I sought out (and I still seek out) those people who play music for themselves, and for each other, for free and for fun, rather than simply satisfying the call for entertainment or music for the tourists. I loved to read Rainer Maria Rilke say, in no uncertain terms, to the young poet, "Don't write unless you have to."

I read and listened to Brendan Breathnach speak about traditional music, song and dance, and I learned a great deal. For example, he wrote in *Folk Music and Dances of Ireland*:

> Genuine traditional players were fast disappearing and the young people attracted to the music were acquiring, by choice, tunes made popular by public performers to the neglect of their local music and under a misapprehension about the virtues of classical tone and techniques, were striving to play in a manner more appropriate to art than to folk music.

I went to Cork to hear the great man from Japan, Dr. Suzuki, speak about music education. He told us that we are all born with music, equal in music, but it is the environment which decides where we go from there. I studied the writings of the great Sufi musician, Inyat Khan, from the early 1900s. My friend and neighbour in Morton Street, New York, Noah Shapiro, introduced me to music of Ancient India, the music of the spheres. At times I have felt very strong connections to the Vina and the Sitar.

Yehudi Menuhin also touched me in his writings about music. I heard him perform in a solo concert in Sydney and it was out of this world. I felt like dancing.

I came across an African proverb which sums up so much for me, *If you can talk, you can sing, if you can walk, you can dance.* I know people today who can't talk, but can sing, and people who can't walk, but can dance.

Sometimes, people assume it's just a matter of picking up an instrument and improvising music or as they say 'having a jam, messing about'. That is not the case at all. There is a whole musical development that has to occur. It takes years of practice to develop technical abilities and a lifetime of practice to connect to the soul of the music.

Over the years I have developed and made use of the gift of teaching, or passing on the music to those that want it, and I am very, very happy about four things in my music life. I am happy that:

🏵 I have spent so long, like years, learning traditional Irish music. I will always be a learner, I hope.

🏵 I learned the music directly from the people that played it all their lives, for the love of it.

🏵 I learned the stories and the social context of the music and songs, in order to fully understand what I am playing and singing.

🏵 I decided to live in music rather than just make a living from music.

I've come up with four directions to living in music. Some people might say these are directions to learning and playing music. Here they are:

🌀 Learn to play music for yourself – it's easier said than done.

🌀 Learn to play with others – listen to learn, learn to listen.

🌀 Learn to play for others – from the inside out.

🌀 Pass it on/give it away – help others in their music-making.

Sin é. A million things can be said about the traditional, but really it's just to play it, or sing it, and walk on, a chara (my friend). Sober and clean music, as long as I'm spared the health.

A DAY OUT IN SLIGO

(John Hoban)

Buskin' in Sligo, one long day in June,
I stepped into a bar to have me a beer.
This old man came in, addressed the company,
Big Georgeen Carmody gave him his chair.

He thanked him, sat down, gathered his senses.
'Yes Sir,' said herself, 'what will it be?'
The old man stayed silent, stood up so gracefully,
just as he spoke his eye fell on me.

'I am a bold tinker,
my name it is Reilly,
I've worked at my trade and it's very well known,
that working cold metal makes a fella grow thirsty,
only for that I'd leave liquor alone.

'So, don't blame a fellow for taking a little.
You know it is right for to moisten the clay.
If you'll believe me, I will not deceive you,
once is enough for your whiskey to pay.'

Slowly he opened his coat and he took out
a brown leather purse with his wealth for the day.
He counted the copper, reached for his measure,
his hands shook, his eyes danced and this he did say.

'Three thousand times over, I've tramped here from Leitrim,
through Boyle, Keadue and Ballinamore.
I never harmed no-one, I asked for no favours,
I found I was welcome at everyone's door.'

He was humming an old jig I'd never heard.
It sounded so lonesome, so high and so clear.
He drained the last drop, bid me adieu,
the song that I've sung has the same tune for you.

Notes on the song:
One fine day in Sligo town, I was having my tea break in Hargadon's pub when the door opened slowly. In came a very tall, stately, elderly gentleman. A Traveller, or knight of the road. After he had said his piece (as written in the song), the bean an tí handed him a glass of whiskey, some copper changed hands, and as far as I could see, he looked and smiled at me, drank back his deoirín (drop) and said goodbye to us all. I could not believe it. I felt blessed. A few moments passed and then I heard a lovely jig running around inside my head, 'The Bold Doherty from the North Country'. I feel as though Reilly sang it, and left it with me. So, this formed the music to the words he spoke. Some years later, it all came back to me, I added a few verses, and I have sang it all over the world in honour of that 'A Day Out in Sligo'. Some other singers in America and Australia have liked the song and asked me if they could sing it. I often remember a friend in Australia, Jimmy Gregory, gone on slí na fírinne (the way of the truth), who loved to sing about Reilly in Sligo.

ACHILL – ONE DAY WITH YOU

(John Hoban)

I hear the sound of the summer breeze,
the helpless cry of a newborn lamb.
A robin sings outside my window,
the mist enshrouds this stony land.

The scent of turf
and bog oak burning.
The rhodedendron now in bloom.
The sea is wild,
with brave white horses,
here in Achill,
one day with you.

Cattle stop and stare at people
as they make their way to the garden green.
Black turf is cut and footed neatly,
with a song and dance, I've heard and seen.

This must be what it's all about, John.
This must be where you started from.
A shooting star
across a frikened pale moon.
Here in Achill,
one day with you.

Notes on the song:
This song is a real favourite of mine. It too came down from Curraun
Hill, to Béal Farsad. As I looked around me, I felt a real strong sense of
harmony, of being connected with nature, and, maybe for the first time,
being fully and really with myself. It was wonderful. 'This must be...' I
never knew before this that I could be with all this natural love, beauty,
life. A moment of clarity, and then it rained for a week. No matter.

Chapter 9

VAN DIEMEN'S LAND

I met two black swans in Queensland one day,
they restored me to sanity, like making hay.
I spent three days by train, across the Nullarbor Plain,
with no tree in sight.
I near went insane.
('Knight of the Road', John Hoban)

I knew, as I looked out on Sydney Harbour during my first visit
to Australia in 1988, that I had been there before. I felt it somewhere deep in my soul, I felt connected. I had been offered a
job teaching and playing music by a community of people that had
decided that the best way to learn Irish music was to bring out a
'live one' from Ireland. I also secured a job playing in a ballad band
called Irish Mist. I kind of enjoyed singing 'The Black Velvet Band',
'The Wild Rover', and such well-known songs to audiences of
young Irish immigrants and people from every corner of the world.
I felt I was starting a new life, a new way. I'd reached the end of the
line in March 1987. Life as I had lived it, and as I knew it, was over.
Providence had another plan and it's still working for me, thankfully, a moment at a time. It's a long story that will have to wait for
another day. Once again, my first language of music was guiding
me 'out foreign altogether', as the old people used to say at home in
Tirawley, North Mayo.

It had always been on the cards that I would travel to foreign
lands as soon as I was old enough to do so. My nomadic, homeless,
wandering existence was directly linked to the loss of my parents at
such a young age, and the loss of my home base. However, I must
say, these were not the only contributing factors. I remember when
I first heard Pete Seeger sing about Montgomery, Alabama, and
the Civil Rights movement in the USA, I would have gone there
if I could have. Hearing the songs of Django Reinhardt, Robert
Johnson, Victor Jara, Memphis Minnie or Delia Murphy, always

made me think about travelling to other places. A foreign land. I couldn't wait to follow the trail of the music which was lighting up my soul and giving all life meaning, creating a sacred path to the four directions.

I worked as a musician/teacher in Sydney, and anywhere else I put my mandocello down in Australia, for six months in '88. I taught people, young and old, how to play Irish music. I played in 'traps' – public houses – with bands and with many fine musicians. I went solo, sang in folk festivals all over, played on the streets of some towns. I brought my music to hospitals, prisons, played in the open air, and gave renditions of old tunes on the Indian-Pacific train as it snaked across the Nullarbor Plain, by day and by night. I learned music and great songs from many people, 'Bare Legged Kate' from John Dengate, 'Stan Tracy's' and 'The Boys of Tandaragee' from Eilis O'Connor, from Dundalk, to name a few. In fact, Eilis and I taught set dancing in Newtown Hall, a suburb of Sydney. This stood us well as we practised the dances we would later perform for 'the wren' or 'the ran' dance on St. Stephen's Day. This was an ancient Irish custom which, I am proud to say, was revived by us in this faraway land. I remember them all, Mort, Pat 'The Piper' Lyons, Cath Taylor, and the stars of the show – the Banner Beauties, Mary Shannon and Teresa McNamara. They danced and played their music on St. Stephen's day, 1991.

When we reached Camperdown
the spirits were high.
The banker, the piper, the abbot close-by.
Lawson, Behan and Shane McGowan,
were in Phil Gannon's pub in
Old Sydney town.
('The Wren in Oz', John Hoban, St. Stephen's Day, 1991)

I met a lot of people from Latin America at the neighbourhood centre in Newtown, Sydney. There were Chileans, Brazilians and Colombians. They got together in a venue called La Peña. I loved to go there to sit, and absorb and learn from their music, language and dance. I felt a very powerful connection with music being played on guitars, charango, quenas and flutes. I felt transported to another world. In a musical sense, I felt that I was a citizen of a great, wonderous world, which was without boundaries and without ownership of anything. We were all the one, passing through, singing our way as we walked our songlines. I made friends with some Aboriginal people, and I loved the way they spoke, and the way they saw life. When they spoke about the land and dreamtime, I felt they were speaking about music. It sounded like the same thing to me. I learned a lot about their horrendous history, and felt great empathy with them, with their lives.

I remember seeing an advertisement in the paper *The Sydney Morning Herald* for a Monday night gig/concert in Pacino's nightclub in Gladesville. The artist was Nusrat Fateh Ali Khan. I could not believe my luck. I went to the gig with another musician, Noirín Coleman, to hear this great man sing. It was an amazing event. Lasted for eight or nine hours, and he was singing for the whole time. All the people present were followers of Qawwali music. Nearly everyone, from infants to ancient people, hailed from Pakistan or India. The experience has never left me, the feeling of this deeply spiritual, inner journey of praise and love in music. I feel it was a glimpse of the beauty which lies ahead, it is probably what heaven sounds like. I don't know. Gladesville, Sydney, one night in December '88. Thank God for music and for life when I think of this event. I was lucky enough to see Nusrat a few more times before he passed on. I saw him perform in New York and London. I could see the two worlds of his music so clearly. I was so happy to have been part of the Pacino's experience. He did this performance for his own people. It was infinite; it was not of this world. It was pure spirit, and I was somehow included in it. The other concerts were just that, concerts, a different world.

I remember taking a two-day journey on board the Indian-Pacific train from Sydney to Perth. I sat next to an elderly lady, her name was Gladys Linnane. I was visiting my sister Carmel, her husband Brian, and daughters Michelle and Kiara, who lived in Perth. Gladys's brother, Paddy, lived in Kalgoorlie, where we parted company. We sang songs in the cheap *sit-up* carriages along with some young kids, real hippies, who were also travelling. They were singing Neil Young and Bob Dylan songs, 'Hurricane', 'All Along the Watchtower', 'Heart of Gold', and 'This is the story of Johnny Rotten, the King is dead but he's not forgotten'! We had a scream. When the train stopped for a break, we went for a stroll in the desert. Gladys knew an awful lot about the plants, birds, and animals of the bush, and she shared her knowledge with us. She also recited poems by my favourite Australian poet, Henry Lawson:

I'm the Mother bush that loves you,
come to me when you are old
('The Night Train', Henry Lawson)

I spent a lovely time spent in Western Australia. One night in Perth, I even got to hear the fourteenth Dalai Lama speaking about wisdom and compassion. It was in a rock'n'roll arena – Midnight Oil and John Cougar Mellencamp were the next gigs. I felt I had been at the Sermon on the Mount. I had a really strong feeling that I had met my teacher, my friend and my leader, I will never forget it. Saol fada (long life) to His Holiness. May peace be with all sentient beings. Peace to Tibet. The Dalai Lama's teachings awaken a place within me, the same place where music touches me. A place of truth and compassion. When I first heard him speak in Perth 1988, I felt I knew him. I can't explain it in words, but maybe this is what I try to do with music. Almost twenty years later, my wife, Isabela, and I, found our way to hear his teachings in his home in exile, a place called Dharamsala, Northern India.

I developed my connection further with Tibet by playing at a concert in the Tibetan Institute of Performing Arts in Dasa (Dharamsala) on 5th March 2007 to celebrate the Tibetan uprising. I sang and played my own songs and then played a duet with the great Tibetan man, Pasang Tsering. I played the fiddle and together we sang 'The Minstrel Boy'. A high point for me in my musical life.

The harp he loved ne'er spoke again,
For he tore its chords asunder.
And said 'no chains shall sully thee
Thou soul of love and bravery.
Thy songs were made for the pure and free.
They shall never sound in slavery.'
(Thomas Moore)

At least one thousand Tibetan monks applauded, roared and cheered us on that evening.

Everywhere I go I make contact with the local people, whether it's Dundalk or Australia. I seek them out, we share music and share our stories of survival. We share our experiences, our strengths and hopes in our own way. Music is the source of life for me, so I am always finding new music through meeting new people on 'the road to happy destiny'. I am often helped by my brothers and sisters, who are like me, recovering from the fallout of various addictions. I hope that I help them too.

Music at this time had begun to speak to me in a new way. A clear, bell-like quality in word and sound which guided me towards a new life. A life similar to the life the Dalai Lama spoke of. A life like I had heard in various musical forms which perhaps I did not understand at first, for example, sean-nós singing, the music of Robert Johnson or Alija Bai Conti, or the poems, as Gaeilge (in Irish), of Caitlín Maude.

There have been times when living in unchartered waters, in the vastness of life itself, that I felt scared. But I always sang and played music, and stayed close to the musical, broken, truth of the life I had been granted. I have always held the belief that further along, I will know all about it, I will have all the answers. Further along, I'll understand why.

I learned so much in Australia during the six months I lived there in '88 and again in '91. I feel so grateful to all the people I met there, and God willin' we will meet up again someday in Nirvana, Valhalla or Doolin, County Clare, where we can sing and dance ourselves into creation.

As I said a while back, I knew for sure – don't ask me how – that I had lived in Australia, Van Diemen's Land, a long time ago. I wonder what was my crime?

THE WREN IN SYDNEY
- THE RAN!

(John Hoban)

The wren, the wren,
the king of all birds.
St. Stephen's day,
was caught in the furze.
Up with the kettle,
down with the pan,
give us a dollar,
to bury the wren!

In the year of our Lord 1991
in Sydney, Australia, the crack had begun.
A band of bold heroes,
decided one day,
to bury the wren,
in the old pagan way.

The first port of call,
was on Taverners Hill,
the dance started up,
led by Margaret and Bill.
Máirtín recited,
Eileen led the way,
through old Sydney Town,
on St. Stephen's Day.

They berthed in five dock,
about half past three.
A car load of mummers,
a strange sight to see,
The Illinois Bar,
became Cahirciveen
as they sang and they danced,
decked in orange and green.

When they reached Camperdown,
their spirits were high,
the banker, the abbot,
the piper close by.
The TV crew came,
from Channel 9.
Saw a horse dance a reel,
without losing time.

Then the two Banner Beauties,
cut loose on the floor.
Brushes, footwork, lipstick galore.
Lawson, Behan and Shane McGowan,
were in the Irishman's pub,
in old Camperdown.

They bid Mr. Gannon,
a fair dinkum adieu,
steered for the city,
the spraoi to renew.
To the Mercantile Bar,
in a place called The Rocks,
danced Caroline, Siobhán,
and the bould Gearóid Fox.

They sank a few schooners,
and midis of blue,
strong tae for the teetotallers,
of which there were few.
No hurry, no worry,
we'll bite Kitty O'Shea,
for the sake of the wren,
on this Stephen's day.

It was there our wren boys
and wren girls had fun.
With Jim on the box,
Anne on the drum,
Brian in the Lancers,
showed Margaret the way,
and the buck from Mayo
was made king for the day.

The last house to visit was in Chippendale,
they march'd down Paddington,
and once more set to sail,
to the Thurless Castle,
to Pat and Maureen,
where they called it a day,
and sank the dreoilín.

So, lads and lassies listen to me,
a chailín, alanna, a stór, mo chroí.
I'm just a wee bird,
but the king of them all.
On each Stephen's day, please answer my call.

The wren, the wren,
the king of all birds,
St. Stephen's day,
got caught in the furze,
up with the kettle,
down with the pan,
give us a dollar,
to bury the wren!

Notes on the song:
Acting in my role of ambassador and teacher of all things
Irish in Australia, I decided to educate the folks about the ancient Irish custom known as 'The Wren on St. Stephen's Day'. A
few natives like the 'Banner Beauties' and Eilis O'Connor knew
the craic. Donning a disguise, dressing like mummers/straw-
boys, off we went to beg for money to help us give the poor
wee bird a proper sendoff. We had a wonderful day. Sweatin'
bullets, singing and dancing. Sydney never saw the likes of it.
It was so inspiring that after hearing me sing this song in San
Francisco in 1992, a bunch of exiles decided to revive/start the
custom in California.

THE OLD QUARTER

(John Hoban)

In Texas tonite,
there shines this strange light.
A wonder to behold,
as I once more give up the fight.

All is deadly silent,
not even the lonesome cricket sound,
confused, content, connected,
today in Houston town, Texas.

What about this weird world we live in,
full of beauty so rare.
For those free gifts of creation,
how little we care.
Oil and the dollar rule the roost,
profit, not people,
everything to lose.
Confused, content, connected,
today in Houston town, Texas.

Rainbows and robins,
self will run riot.
Green fields and yellow corn,
adios Mexico.

Listening to Townes Van Zandt,
Lightning Hopkins and Freddy Fender,
wasted days and wasted nights.

All my short life,
listening with my heart,
at the Old Quarter,
today in Houston town, Texas.

Notes on the song:
A strange little poem/song written about a hot summer's
evening while my wife Isabela and I were visiting her family,
who at the time, where living in Houston, Texas. Just thoughts
really, about hummingbirds, crickets, Townes Van Zandt, and
a few other things. Adios Mexico.

Chapter 10

TURTLE ISLAND – USA

It was great to arrive in New Mexico.
To be met off the bus by a gent from Mayo.
We made music for cowboys and the Indians too,
we 'saddled the pony' for the Navajo and Sioux.
('Knight of the Road', John Hoban)

Where to begin with the USA? With a song maybe? So many, too many to sing. Woody Guthrie's 'Do, Re, Mi', perhaps? I have such a connection with this country, in so many different ways. Many of my relatives, on my father's side, travelled west from Cobh in Cork and Rinanna in County Clare to find themselves in Idlewild, New York, and on Ellis Island. After these first stops, they spread out further to places such as the Carolinas, Cleveland, Ohio and God knows where else, roasting and freezing, and diggin' for gold perhaps.

We always had Yanks as visitors when we were small. Brooklyn was more real to me than Ballina. Bing Crosby and Al Jolson songs were more popular than our own native songs, 'The songs our fathers loved', as *The Walton's* radio show used to announce. Most of my father's people headed for the USA, but some stayed at home. His brothers Tommy, Thady and Johnny were priests in Brooklyn, one other brother, Josie, was an engineer in Dublin. His sister Mary B. was a nun, a Reverend Mother in North Carolina, I believe. Another sister, Patricia, was a nurse in New York, and another, Sally, kept the home fires burning in Carrabán, Westport. So every now and then the Yanks would dock at 'Belmont', even the name of our house was called after a spot in the Carolinas, where the Mercy Convent was located. Oh Mercy! When they arrived, we traded gifts. A parcel of the latest US fashion, usually pyjamas for the kids. The kids would then be brought into the parlour to sing our little hearts out. We sang a rebel song or 'The West's Awake' (I had no idea what it was about), 'Hail Glorious Saint Patrick', or maybe a hymn. A tear or two might fall onto the red carpet. The air smelled of brandy and Lucky Strikes. I enjoyed the wee gig. When the TV arrived in the late '60s, I was able to see where it was all happening and where all the Yanks lived. I never felt any connection to the Irish-American world of the Kennedys, *The Quiet Man*, Maureen and the Duke, despite how they inspired such respect and enthusiasm from most of the Irish Diaspora in that part of the world.

My experience of New York felt the same as my experience of learning music – there was no learning needed, just the fingers needed to toughen up and find their way. I once asked my friend, James O'Malley, how he learned music. He told me he listened really close to the song over a long period of time until it came into his fingers. It works the same way for me.

Listening is the key to learning music. A lot of people don't actually listen to music anymore, they just sort of hear music with the radio on in the background, in traffic, Midwest or Lyric FM, and all stations in between. Droning away. Actually listening to music is a totally different experience. It's about feeling the music, moving with it internally, trying to understand it emotionally, clearing the mind to allow the sounds and the voice to work their magic. No thought process, no criticism. It's a beautiful way to learn music. It's quite difficult, but it must be developed in order to learn music, and certainly in order to join in with other people in music. It's all about respecting music for itself. Respecting and wondering about the gift of music. I've seen great musicians do this and they are great listeners.

As a youngster I heard this song,

From the New York Island
to the gulf stream waters.
From the Redwood forest in California,
this land was made for you and me.
('This land is your land', Woodie Guthrie)

118

I also heard about Sacco and Vanzetti, two Italian immigrants who were wrongly executed, in a song by Woody Guthrie. I heard the songs 'Deportees' and 'Dust Bowl Refugees'. Around this same time, LPs by The Weavers and the Almanac Singers made their way to me. I remember hearing Alan Lomax's interview with Woody Guthrie in Oklahoma in the '40s. It was so funny to me. Every sentence started with 'Well...'

My education in American music continued during every step of my journey in the States. My very good friend and neighbour, Noah Shapiro, introduced me to Lower and Upper Manhattan. We went to see Snooks Eaglin, Ruben Gonzales, Bob Dylan, Booker T and the M.G.s, and many more. We had many's the great nosh/feeds together in Chinatown and in Kenny Shopsin's, Greenwich Village. The Beat Scene, the folk scene, the '60s art scene, you name it, it was all there. I love the eerie inner silence I experience in New York. I am sure New York is alive. It is like a personal friend, an addict, a refugee, a power of senses and sights. A heavenly father, perhaps.

People from every corner of the world come to Manhattan Island, the Lower East Side. All outsiders. All trying to live in New York. I feel like I am an original in New York, never afraid, never sure, always a blast or a blas (taste) of a song coming to me:

My feet are here on Broadway, this blessed harvest morn...
('The Old Bog Road', Traditional)

One night, many moons ago, I went to hear Andy McGann play in Tom Reilly's bar on Lexington Avenue in Manhattan. I was pushed up onstage to play and sing a few songs with my bouzouki which I bought in the Humbert Inn, Castlebar. I sang and played, and Andy invited me to play the next weekend there with him. I was over the moon. It went really well apart from the crowd showing us no appreciation. Andy loved when I launched into a Jimmy Rodgers' song, 'Rough and Rowdy'. He laughed and played wonderful fiddle music. I heard everything I needed, or dreamed of, when hearing him playing, including the music of poor Michael Coleman. Coleman left Ireland in

1914 having learned music in his native Sligo from neighbours like Philip O'Beirne, P.J. McDermott, and Johnny Gorman, a travelling piper from Roscommon. His recordings of traditional music influenced and changed Irish music at home and abroad. He died in 1945 and is buried in the Bronx. Andy learned from Coleman when he was a young boy growing up in New York. It was a huge privilege being included in the lineage of Coleman's greatness. I never met Andy after those nights, but I hear his music always, forever I would say.

I also came across Pete Seeger in upstate New York, dancing a half-set with his wife and another couple on board *The Woody Guthrie*, a sort of tug boat on the Hudson River. I met Doc Watson and his son Merle in the Bottom Line bar, I had a good drink with Merle that night. I saw Patti Smith and Lou Reed in the Village hanging out. I heard Kerouac, Ginsberg and Co. on McDougal Street, and even thought I heard the Clancy Brothers, Brendan Behan and Dylan Thomas belting out 'The Croppy Boy' in the White Horse bar on Hudson Street. Perhaps it was a dream, an illusion.

I always love the spirit of New York. I love the humour and the honesty of the people. Most of all I love the sheer sense of music that I feel whenever I am privileged to be in the middle of it, just walking through the city and listening. When we got the black and white television in 1966, one of the first programmes to make its way into our sitting room was *Car 54* – the tale of two New York cops, Toody and Muldoon, and their escapades. It was a howl. The words in the theme song went like this, 'There's a traffic jam in Harlem that's backed-up to Jackson Heights. Car 54, where are you?' As kids, we used to go around the house singing this refrain.

My friend Noah told me a story about witnessing a woman freaking out on a bus one day, poor crayture. Noah told me that the bus driver turned to her and said very kindly, "There is no point in going bananas in the big apple. You will only end up in the fruit bowl." That line should be in a song. New York, start spreading the news, so good they named it twice, as Mr. Frank Sinatra said.

New York is one of my favourite places on this planet. I love to be there. Very often, I think of myself, musically and in other ways, as being somewhere between Lower Manhattan, and Clare Island. Both places have a similar effect on me, a kindred music quality or inspiration. A very powerful sense of silence comes over me in New York, a silence that transcends the noise of the living city. This sensation helps me to gain an understanding of just how and why all this great music, art, and people-culture evolve here on this island. Silence is the foundation of all music. I feel sure the Native people who lived on Manhattan Island gave this place a wonderful music-life because I can still hear it. I feel a sense of certainty of my place in the big picture when I walk and sing and listen in New York. I go there as often as I can. It's a yearly pilgrimage for me, and more if I can manage it.

San Francisco is another wonderful place for me to visit because of the sea and The Mission district. I love to think of what it was like in the '50s with the Beat stuff in North Beach, and the '60s with the Summer of Love, The Grateful Dead and Haight Ashbury. I visit my friends all over the city, High Noon, The Dry Dock, The Skid Row, Tenderloin, these are all places in San Francisco. The city is divided into districts of all kinds of diversity, cultures and people. I recorded a song in Hyde Street Studio, and then I lost it, so I don't really know what it sounded like.

I am happy to report that we managed to revive the custom of 'The Wren' in San Francisco in much the same way we did in Sydney. We started it in 1992, dressed to kill, disguised, singing and dancing in various locations in San Francisco. The 'Doc', Noel Gantly, was made king for the day.

For the first ten minutes keep it on the ground
as we make our way 'round 'Frisco town.
The Wren, the wren, king of all birds,
St. Stephen's day got caught in the furze.
Up with the kettle, down with the pan,
give us a dollar to bury the wren!
('The Wren', John Hoban)

I love the song Hank Snow sings – 'I've Been Everywhere' – because that's what it feels like at times. I continue my songline/journey to the town of Detroit. This is where the most important thing in my life happened – I met my wife Isabela on Thanksgiving Day 1995, right there, in downtown Detroit, in Motown. We met at a party and we became instant friends. We started 'walking out', as they say in Ireland, and we were married in Castlebar in 1999. We are living happily ever after, that's the truth. She is the best artist I have ever met, and we now play music together, which is a total joy and expression of everything that is new and old. Peru is her home country. We have visited there, and we have felt the music, the dance and the language in a very profound, homely and beautiful way. When we landed in Lima, I felt at home immediately. I absolutely loved the feel, the vibe, and the look of both Lima and the Andes.

Detroit itself is a marvel. It is also a contradiction such as the American Dream, huge wealth and massive poverty side by side, the racial tensions and all that. I will never forget the feeling I got when I first stood in the Motown recording studio. My whole body was shaking as I remembered my childhood in Mayo listening to all the great stars who recorded their songs on this very spot: Marvin Gaye, Stevie Wonder, The Vandellas, The Supremes, The Miracles, The Jackson family, Aretha Franklin, such talent. They all came from the Projects – poorer housing – around the corner from the Motown recording studio, all local kids.

I have a huge interest in music history, where the people were at, where the inspiration came from, how they lived. I have yet to visit Memphis, Tennessee, and Parchment Farm, Mississippi State penitentiary where Eddie James, known as Son House, was living for a while. I don't know how I first got to hear about Son House, but I am a real fan of his music, have been all my life.

Muddy Waters said that when he was growing up in music, Son House was the king. Muddy reckoned that if it wasn't for Son House he wouldn't have played music. 'Preachin' the Blues', 'Dry Spell Blues', 'Low Down Dirty Dog blues...' I used to think about that, imagine Muddy Waters not playing music, I'd have the blues forever.

I also thought a lot about how Django Reinhardt badly damaged two of his fingers in a caravan fire when he was eighteen years old. He then went on to learn the guitar all over again, but even better than before, using only two fingers for solos. Both Django and Grapelli were Aquarians, water carriers. Grapelli was an aristocrat (whatever that is when it's at home) and Django, a gypsy, who has no home. I met a first cousin of Django's in a jazz club in Bonn, Germany in the early '80s. He could make the guitar talk. We got on famously, had a few, then parted ways. He was an amazing singer as well as guitar virtuoso. He knew all about Ireland, horses and blacksmiths. I often wonder what became of him. He is in a great movie that I have seen quite a few times, *Latcho Drom*. The movie had a huge impact on me. It was made by Tony Gaitlif and it told the tale of the journey of Roma from India to Europe, represented in various music forms.

I seem to have a connection with this film because I have also met and played the mandocello with another man who appears in the movie. He too is a gypsy who earns his living playing in Istanbul with his son, who is an extraordinary singer and drummer. The man plays the fiddle and he sings. I met the two of them busking in a café under the Galatian Bridge, performing for a band of locals who listened closely, while drinking raki, and sang along. It was awesome. We had no words that we could exchange, but for about an hour and a half, we played a very strange and wonderful brand of ceol/music. We were friends straight away. We felt safe; we felt at home. I have always felt sure that music comes from the gypsy world, from the nomadic, rather than from the world of settlers.

My friend Tony and I went to Istanbul to visit Johnny Mulhern, his wife Cathy, and family Dara, Ruth and Brendan. We had a great holiday, especially playing music in the amphitheatre in Efes, and playing to curious Japanese tourists, and a few Turks also. We ended up being stranded in Kuşadasi because the airline that carried us out went broke and out of business. Mayo was playing Cork in the All-Ireland football final, they were beat, of course. But I wrote a song for Willie Joe, the footballer, one of the finest sons of Mayo, and sang it for him once in his pub in Castlebar. We got home eventually, it all worked out in the end, as it always does.

The Turks are a pious people,
they pray five times a day.
We met the twelve Apostles
gutting fish along the quay.
In a Turkish bath, a 'hammam',
we were scrubbed from head to toe.
We were the two cleanest lads
that ever left Mayo.
I don't know, maybe so,
but no one here has heard of Willie Joe!
('Willie Joe', John Hoban 1989)

Johnny and his good friend Wally Page, are the two finest songwriters and singers I have ever met. They are also great blokes. They play a brand of music that I would always follow, I'd stand in the snow to hear them play. Long may they sing those songs. It's no harm to let them at it, as the saying goes.

Hank Williams and Professor Longhair are two music people who called to my door, moved in, and have never left. I can't describe the sense of timelessness I experience with the music world of Hank, the crayture. I believe every word he sings, and feel every note he plays. I keep finding new songs by Hank, and they transport me to that world again.

My wife and I befriended a Japanese Soto Zen monk, Venerable Raido Kimura, when visiting a Cistercian monastery in the South of Ireland. He was over here studying the monastic way in Mount Melleray. He used to meet up with us and help us so much by sharing his wisdom and kindness. We covered all topics. One day we moved into the world of music and chant. I never will forget this man's face as he looked at me and asked did I like to listen to Hank Williams sing? He said he thinks that Hank Williams is a real artist, and he wears a bow tie and dresses so well. Japan, a Zen monk and Hank.

Professor Longhair, or Fess as he is also known, came to me via my friend, Noah. The sound of his music, his way, drew me in immediately, and always when I listen to him, I am rooted to the spot. I almost feel afraid to breathe in case I miss a sound. I'd love to sit beside him and hear him knock out some rock'n'roll gumbo or 'Tipitina'. He was, and is, so free. Just like his name says, Henry Roland Byrd.

All over the USA, the music traced and followed the invisible map that I hold inside me, the songline. The same songline I spoke of experiencing with the Aboriginal people in Australia. It is an inner musical score, mapping out places, locations and states of being that I must visit in order to heal myself, and others, by sound and by self-forgetting.

So, in all the places that I have visited along the way, the only reality for me, and indeed the only reason for me to be present, is the song or piece of music. It's this way all my life, everywhere I've ever been. A mystery to me, but I'm sure the manager knows the story.

My travels throughout the USA have brought me to many places. I loved Galveston Island, New Mexico, California, Green Bay, Lambeau, where I saw the Packers and The Bears slug it out. I have been to San Antonio, Texas, the home of the band, The Tornados and their famous brand of tex-mex songs such as 'Adios Mexico', and 'Guacamole'.

I have a special grá (love) for Connecticut. My good friend Joey Moran from Curraun, Achill moved there and brought me out to teach a small group of people in Fairfield, Connecticut in the early '90s. They call themselves The Shamrogues. Over the years, The Shamrogues have grown into a fine orchestra of traditional Irish music and song. Every year since, I visit them and we have become great friends as the music grows fiercer. The Burnetts look after us well when we are there. Joey loved the song 'Farewell to the Gold', so he once made a trip to New Zealand, and he sent me a postcard from the Shotover river telling me that he was having no luck panning for gold. Joey has passed on and when I sing the song, I remember him:

Shotover river, your gold it is waning,
and it's years since the colour I've seen.
There's no use just sitting
and lady luck blaming,
I'll pack up and make the break clean.
('Farewell to the Gold', Traditional)

Houston, Texas, is a town I have often visited and have grown to love. My wife lived there at one time. So did Townes Van Zandt. He, too, is part of my songline. I listened to his records in Dublin in the 1970s, and went on to meet him in the Róisín Dubh club in Galway in 1997. I bought him a drink before he went on stage, for the last time in Galway as this was near the end of his short life. He certainly struck many's a chord with me. When we met he was alone, shaking but smiling and he said to me, "Can you give me a hand out?" It wasn't about money, it was about a recognition of each other, a kinship even though we had never met before. I thanked him for his music and I shared a bit of my story with him. He had his drink, told me he enjoyed our time chatting, then he played and sang for an hour or so. I am so glad I was there. I sat on my own, and there were about ten other people in the club. I will never forget who I heard singing that night, and the man who wrote 'You Are Not Needed Now', 'White Freight Liner', and 'Waiting Around to Die'.

North America, or Turtle Island, has inspired me all my life. This inspiration has come from many quarters, from the Brooklyn visitors and the Carolinas, to the Native Modoc/Klamath/Karuk people I know in Oregon, Mount Shasta in the West. I especially love the Native people. Their way of being makes sense to me. I also identify strongly with the Elders, they are great people, Black Elk, Fools Crow, Geronimo, Crazy Horse and Red Hawk. I have a close connection with the Choctaw people of Oklahoma. Our histories merge in the not too distant past. The Choctaw people have strong connections with all of us here in Mayo, in Dubh Loch. In 1847 the Choctaw people heard of the Dubh Loch Tragedy, when hundreds of Irish people died while crossing the Mayo mountains in search of food during the Famine. They gathered $710 US and sent it to help the suffering Irish people. Let us not forget that these people did this when they were suffering from their own 'Trail of Tears'.

My father brought us to Dubh Loch as children, told us the stories of the Drochshaoil (the Famine, the Bad Life), showed us the bleached bones piled high in mass graves on the Talamh Bán (white ground) beyond Louisburgh. I remember those people, my own ancestors, always in song and in my soul.

What a great life this is, songs to warm the heart, songs to show the way and songs to question all that is important. Gift ó Dhia (from God), as Micho Russell said once to me.

THE CURRAUN SONG

(John Hoban)

I've travelled the world from the east to the west.
Playing my music, turning a song.
I've been on all kinds of roads, botharíns, dirt tracks,
you name it, I've been there before.
As soon as we reach Mulranny town,
turn left at the church, pass the school,
the heart fills with joy, with wonder and awe.
As we make our way to Curraun.

It's some road so it is by the shores of Clew Bay.
Gaze at Croagh Patrick so high.
Cliara, Turk, Bofin below,
it'd make any grown pilgrim cry.
As soon as we reach dear Poll-a-Rick,
we feel we're already home, our
hearts fill with joy, wonder and awe,
as we make our way to Curraun.

You step into The George, smell the turf fire,
you're greeted with handshake and smile.
"Sé do bheatha tá fáilte romhat,
suigh síos, lig do scíth for a while."
We have a glass, exchange the news,
a sing-song starts up right away.
'The Rocks of Bawn', 'The Foggy Dew',
We used to sail 'round Clew Bay.

'Major John', 'Mulranny Town', 'Shanagolden' also.
'Cúil na mBinn', 'The Youth of Mayo'
and of course 'The May Morning Dew'.
'Dan O'Hara', 'Michael Hayes', 'Dangerous Dan McGrew',
'Behind the Bush in the Garden',
'My old Home in Mayo', too.
'My Lagan Love', 'Moonlight in Mayo',
'A Lady That's Known As Lou'.
Mick Flanagan 'the great', God rest his soul,
'The Red River Valley' too. 'All the Ways to Galway'
John Jim miming a jig.
'The Lakes of Ponchatrain' is being sung
"Ciúnas, one voice please."

Everyone here has a song to sing,
everyone listens so well.
The melodeon is passed from a hand to a hand,
and it too weaves its own spell.
Football's discussed with a passion so fine,
as is turf, the aimsir and hay.
We're great, so we are, to be here at all,
with such nature by the shores of Clew Bay.

We crossed over one time to Cliara so fine,
in a vessel called *Banríon an Ghleanna*.
We were friends on land, enemies at sea.
To the home of the Great Grainne Uaile.
We drank plenty, played music, pulled tug-of-war,
danced half-sets in Bernard's till dawn.
Just how we got back to sweet Ath an Aoil.
It was all a great mystery to me.

Now to conclude, to finish my song,
let me sing to you one and all,
I've hit the deck, so I have many times
but I got up after each fall.
No matter where I ever wander,
no matter what punches are thrown,
my heart and my heels will le cúnamh Dé,
make my way to Curraun.

Notes on the song:
Thanks to John Gallagher, we ended up in The George, 'the big house', in Curraun on the night of an ordination celebration of a priest from Castlebar. It was in the 1970s. I had returned from Camden Town for the event. So, to be in such a wonderful place and playing music was like being in heaven, on the shores of Clew Bay. This song remembers fondly, and gives thanks to all those people, those days and that music. The Curraun people are all 'in the know' of who sang what. God be good to them all. Ní bheidh ár leithéidí arís ann (our likes will not be around again). Hopefully!

CIARÓG EILE

(John Hoban)

My name is Mary Hoban,
also known as Ciaróg Eile.
Born in Connacht - Ireland,
raised in West Tyrone.
My family deserted me,
the old man joined the navy,
my gran lived till 93,
she sang her rebel songs.

19 hundred and 54, I heard tell of Memphis, Tennessee.
They spoke of Sun Records, The Killer and young Presley.
I'm no bad flute player myself,
I learned from John McKenna,
I bid farewell to Pomeroy,
and head for Mexico.

The streets were no more paved with gold,
but for the Hopi, I'd have died of cold.
They fed us whiskey and dried beans,
gave me the sraideog for the night.
Bit by bit, I made my way, played the flute for an honest pay.
As I heard a woman say one time,
'Anything is better than the rain.'

My best mate was a boy named Jim,
six foot four, horrid thin, he clocked a man in Juarez,
we hightailed it out of town.
He'd come home from somewhere back East,
Lordship, Cooley or Kilcreest,
he hurled for Behy le cheile,
he danced to the old Ballinakill.
Now to conclude and to end my song,
I never did anybody wrong.

I played the flute, made my way,
and fitted in nowhere.
So good luck, adios, a chairde go léir.
Keep the faith and never fear.
Just remember in all fairness,
aithnionn ciaróg ciaróg eile.
It takes one to know one, she smiled.

Notes on the song:
This song written as a tribute to one of my all-time favourite singers/musicians, Jimmy Rodgers, 'The Singing Brakeman'. Not sure how I first heard his music but it certainly has stuck with me. On a plane to California from New York, I started thinking, dreaming about Tyrone, dustbowl times and refugees, rebel songs and hurling in the Parish of Behy, South Galway, Hopi Indian prophesies and ways, and famous Céilí bands in the West of Ireland. When I awoke I was in California, '...many miles from Spancil Hill'. Isn't it marvellous how these songs appear out of nowhere.

Chapter 11

TROUBADOUR, TEACHER, MUSICIAN

I've walked these roads for eighty-odd years.
Between the rose and the heather.
('Between the Rose and the Heather', John Hoban)

I t's hard to put all my life experiences in a nutshell. It has
become clearer to me by the day, clear as crystal, that music
has shown me a way to live. A way to go. Music continues
to teach and inspire me, to guide and direct my thoughts and
actions, and most of all, it shows me where I am in creation.

As I grow older in music, it becomes richer and easier in many
ways. Naturally, through years of practice, I have become more
adept and skilled in the technical aspects of music. Of course there
is more to music than technique and rules. At the end of the day,
it's the feelings of the singer, the song and the listener all coming together which create the magic and the sense of wonder. Music to me
is an awful lot about friendship, fellowship, kinship and listening to
each other. I believe there are four stages of music:

* Talking, singing or playing.
* Listening, with an open heart (no judgment or criticism).
* Processing, meditation.
* Responding, the action, playing in response.

I have developed a great sense of gratitude for the many gifts
I have been granted. I am beginning to understand that it was
humility, kindness and integrity that I saw in those kind music people I encountered along life's pathway. I also see now,
so clearly, how the mixing of music with the use of alcohol/
intoxicants/chemicals was hellish for me. Perhaps it works for
other people, but as I've said all along, I can only tell my own
story and allow others to do whatever works for them. I do not
express opinions or ideas about other people's music. Of course,

people ask me what I think of so and so as a singer, musician etc., I now answer with, "I don't think. I don't have an opinion on others' music." I let my heart decide, and for me, that is a personal, private place. I speak freely of what inspires me in music, art and life, but I believe the old expression *If you can't say a good word, don't say a bad word.* Just letting go of old ideas and opinions allows me to live a much better life, free from the burden of having to defend my own views, or oppose the views of others. Nothing to prove. Free from expectations and free from opinions, at least for the time being.

I have learned to live one day at a time. I have discovered that I can feel very free in myself and in my music providing I do certain practices which I have developed over the years. It's all to do with the spirit and dealing with my thinking, and perceptions of life. For me, it is like letting go completely of ideas about music/life. It's about being free to live in the moment. Not to be driven or controlled by the past or the future. In music, it involves singing or playing without any expectations about the outcome. It's quite like living and dying in a sea of music, vibration, and truth. It's very simple to me, but I find it difficult to describe this state of being in words.

Intoxicants made this peace and truth impossible for me to reach, mostly because it turned me into a slave to outer conditions, for example, people, places, things, audiences, venues. Alcohol and its allies helped me to cope with the often harsh, and sometimes dangerous, realities of my existence. I used substances which made me sick, and also helped me block out whatever my reality was during these times. Unfortunately, it also made me block out love and life. Not today, by the grace of God. Not for many's the long day, thankfully.

In school, I remember identifying with poor Antoine Raifteirí, the blind poet. I knew him, I was him, a victim, an artist, even though he lived his short life in the 1800s. He was born in Cill Aodhain, near Kiltimagh, County Mayo. He was banished from the area by the landlord for reputedly stealing a horse. He made his way to County Galway where he composed, and played his music on the fiddle for the rest of his life.

136

Mise Raifteirí an File: I am Raftery the Poet

Mise Raifteirí an file,
lán dóchas is grá,
le súile gan solas,
le ciúnas gan chrá.

'Dul siar ar m'aistear
le solas mo chroí,
fann agus tuirseach
go deireadh mo shlí

Féach anois mé
is mo chúl le balla,
ag seinm ceoil
do phócaí folmha

I am Raftery the poet,
full of hope and love,
with eyes without light,
calm without anguish.

Going back in my travels
with the light of my heart,
weary and tired,
to the end of my journey

Look at me now
and my back to the wall,
playing music
to empty pockets.

When I sing these words today, or when I play the fiddle, I feel a sense of celebration in life. I feel I am one with Raifteirí. I honour his life, and I honour my own life because I am sober and clean. It is everything. A friend once said to me, "We know a new happiness and a peace we'd never have known. We will not regret the past nor wish to shut the door on it."

It means so much to me to be able to sing, to play and pass on music without chains, baggage and resentments. Just sweet, raw, truthful music. These days, I live in music without the fear of being found out, or the fear of being five pence short, or the hideous fear of not being good enough to be myself. I won't die trying to be some other imitation in order to be seen to be successful. Reminds me of standing outside the church in November for Sunday Mass – just in case there might be a grain of truth in what the preacher says.

My life in music has led me to work in the world of community arts and music. I like to think of this as service, serving others in the community. I first remember hearing of St. Francis of Assisi's concept in St. Jarlath's, of all places, "It's better to understand than to be understood, better to console than to be consoled, better to love than to be loved." St. Francis, a fiddle player too, I believe.

For many years I have been travelling around Mayo bringing my music to small groups of people gathered in houses, halls, community centres, old schoolhouses, from Blacksod to Ballindine, from Knock to Killadoon, from Keenagh to Achill. Imagine hearing a woman from Achill, now in her nineties, sing 'Somewhere Over the Rainbow' for you each Tuesday, for years. And then to see a man from Ballycroy, in his hundredth year, dancing with a lady to 'Moonlight in Mayo'. It is great to hear him explain, after being complimented on his dancing, that "You have to do what you can for the old people!" Of course, his dancing partner is younger than himself. The truth. What more needs to be said there except, "Dance on, my friends!" Set free by the truth, no doubt

Music-making, singing and teaching have led me from community to community. It has always been the same with me. I suppose this started for me many years ago with the family in summertime, singing as we visited the relatives and the country people. Then came the choir, the church and the hospitals in the '60s in Castlebar, the operas in Tuam, *The Gondoliers*, the White Horse Inn, *Oliver*, off to Dublin and London with outcasts, hipppies, navvies on the line, us all on cheap wine,

Rastas in Notting Hill, Latin Americans in the Troubadour, folk clubs and the Irish ghettos of Kilburn, Putney and North London, and so on. My travels always brought me into contact with rebels, and different sorts of people who took refuge in music and drink and various other cultural activities. When I first started teaching music, I discovered great communities in places like Dundalk, The Cooley Penninsula, and all over Mayo, especially Curraun in Achill. My music also brought me to Cliara, or Clare Island, which I always loved to visit.

In more recent years, I have become very involved in recording the songs and stories of the older people with whom I come into contact. I also work a lot with some very special, wonderful people who have various types of disabilities. These people are very musical, and they express it in very powerful, individual ways. I also work, musically, with people who are recovering from various life-threating addictions. They find that music provides them with a road back to being themselves. Everybody deserves music, and everybody has music, or a love of music, deep in their hearts. So, I do my best to listen and sing for everybody and anybody.

I have alluded to the fact that I have come close, very close, to dying many times in my life. Death has been part of my life from my early days, from losing my grandparents, parents and quite a few friends when I was young, right up to today. I have known a fair share of grief and loss but I have never felt like a victim, and I have never felt sorry for myself. I have always viewed death as just the other side of the coin – the other side of life. I have always felt a real closeness with the next world and with the spirits who have completed their work in this place. I feel certain that we all pass on when we are ready, and that our time here is for learning, and preparing for the next phase. Music and song help me with this way of living. On quite a few occasions, people nearing the end of their lives on earth have specifically requested that I play for them when they are ready to go to the next world. Others have requested that I sing or play at their funerals. I naturally associate songs with people and places, this association eternalises the person with the song. The song and the spirit become one. It's true. It's love, I guess. But what a privilege to be asked to play somebody into the next world. No greater feeling could I have in my musical life.

I always come back to music-making and the need for mutuality and sharing. The musician and the listener, the call and the response, from the heart, to the heart. A man once said to me on Clare Island that, "People have lost the ability to listen. When we were young, we had no choice but to listen to everything." I knew what he meant, as I too have learned that freedom for me is absence of choice. I learn each day that listening is meditation, and that speaking or singing is a prayer. There is an Irish proverb *Is fearr port ná paidir* (a jig is better than a prayer). Nowadays, forming friendships and true relations with people is music to my heart. In my life I have learned, through being involved with various communities, that it is really important not to play music *at* people. In order to learn this we must:

First, develop the relationship over a long time. A friendship and conversation over many days, many years in fact. This relationship extends to the wider community of family and friends.

Second, develop the music relationship. This means knowing the songs, dances, stories, recitations of the particular area and of a particular era. We must bring out the tradition and encourage the sharing of that tradition. Therefore, a true community musician must do a lot of research and learning, and have great musical flexibility in order to be relevant and to be welcomed into the community. This is the way we can be genuinely helpful to each and to any specific community/locality.

Once again, people don't want music forced on them or played at them. Their own traditions and their own lives must be respected and preserved.

The musician must love this work and see its great value. Over decades, I have been enriched beyond words by various communities: the elderly in rural and urban locations and in their homes and care settings, the many people with physical and intellectual disabilities, refugees and asylum seekers, the youth, and people from all walks of life. Without exception, I have received as much, and more, than I have given.

Playing music on the street provides a great theatre space in which to explore the inner and the outer worlds of music-making. Sometimes it can be a difficult or hard station as passers-by divide into those who celebrate music, and those who turn away from it. I have spoken a lot about busking or playing music on the street. I have busked in Sligo, New York, Sydney, Toronto and in many other places, but probably the hardest town of all in which to busk is Castlebar. The home turf. It does require fairly strong resolve in the world of the spirit, a totally shameless approach, and a good sense of humour! People love to see you at it, or else they duck down alleyways conveniently realising they've forgotten something really important so they have to double back. But in general, people love to hear music on the street. I think so anyway.

Songwriting is life itself, storytelling, turning it out. Songs to me feel like spirits, like guardian angels floating around, unseen until the time is right, and suddenly, there they are. Wanting to be sung. Like flowers waiting to blossom. Then there are the other songs, the songs which take a long time to come out, the songs which require a lot of nurturing. This is a deeply personal experience for me. These days I do not worry about what others think of them, or what will the neighbours say, not that it ever really mattered.

The first song that consciously called to me was the 'Long Forgotten Saint'. It is about my mother's passing in 1967. In this song I thank her for giving me life, and for letting me go. It first came to me in or around summer 1970 as I was walking home to Auburn Avenue in Dublin, after a Shamrock Rovers soccer match. I recall singing it in some form or other as I walked through Ranelagh Village, the song just came to me. The next song I experienced in this same way was 'A Day Out in Sligo'.

In the '70s, after my return from London, I made my living by doing the very odd gig (in odd places, with odd people like me), teaching a few pupils, and busking. Very few people were busking in those times, except in Galway where the tradition was carried on by a few older musicians like the Dunnes. Dublin, Belfast and Cork had a tradition of buskers on the streets too. I loved to stand on a street in Wexford, Kerry, Galway, Dundalk, Dublin and Sligo town. I'd play traditional music on the banjo, sometimes sing a ballad or two, and people would drop a few coins into the hat so that I'd have enough to live on for the day. Sometimes I would be joined by another musican, but mostly it was a solo job.

So how does it work? I am often asked which comes first, the words or the music? Which comes first, the hen or the egg? I think a song is like the breath of life, it has to come out, be exhaled, a sigh, a scream. Before it comes out, something first needs to be brought inside, to be inhaled – an experience, a story, a feeling, then just sing it out in the rhythm that comes with the words. Children do this all the time. Watch them as they make up songs when just looking at the sky, or singing to a toy, or when they are looking out the back window of a car. They sing what they see.

The next step is to write it down, sometimes over and over again. Put a chord or two, or three, around it. Record it, tape it, and sit back and listen to it with your heart. When performing music, I feel the background story to the music must be presented to the listener to allow him or her make full sense of it. I am sure it is the same with dance and dance music. It is important that the song is introduced simply, and from the heart, to welcome, and allow the listener into the song. Music must be listened to as the first language of our hearts. No place for judgement, competition, or criticism. I don't have to like every song or piece of music I hear, but I must respect it. We are all people, all songs, all inter-connected. I have learned to accept that I am exactly where I am meant to be in my music. No better and no worse than anybody else. I remember Tommy Potts, the wonderful man and musician from The Liberties in Dublin say in an interview on the radio, "My music is a poor reflection of what's to come." I was amazed. I met him twice, by chance, in the Four Seasons in Capel Street in Dublin, and he played a few tunes on a fiddle for a small while. I felt blessed to have met him in person. His music still inspires me as I try to make the best of my life and my own music, le cúnamh Dé (with God's help). One moment at a time.

The professional world of work and music are very far removed from the world of music in which I now live. I see my world as a moment in time, to sing or play as the music inspires. I have never felt that music should be about having to perform to order or demands. I recall a singer once saying to a person in the audience who was demanding a particular song, "I'm not a jukebox, you know!" I found it highly amusing.

I feel very free at last in music to be myself. I also enjoy making music with many people, too numerous to mention, but I'm sure they know who I am speaking about. I also feel I am just beginning in this life, and I will try to be open to learning from others and from myself, each day.

With a song in your heart,
a breath still in your body,
all you've got to do is walk on!
Walk on, my friend!
('Walk On', John Hoban)

JOE AND LORD GORDON

(John Hoban)

I'm fairly sure, nobody knows, what's going on,
when I play Lord Gordon's reel.
So let me tell you.

Joe and I met, playing in a céilí, in the '70s,
gallons of tae and Sweet Afton,
flowing gently.

Many days later and I flying to Achill,
I stopped and gave to Joe, Lord Gordon's reel,
on the melodeon.

On my way back East, the following day,
I called to visit Joe, as I used to do
fair and easy.

'Have I got it right?' sez he to me,
and proceeded to play Lord Gordon's reel
on the melodeon.

It was the finest setting I'd ever heard.
It put me in mind of a tropical bird,
sweet music, soul music.

There was always fish on a Friday.
There was always a welcome for I,
regardless of how I was travelling.
There was always music,
friendship and neighbours in Joe's house,
night or day.

This goes on and on and on and on,
whenever I play Lord Gordon's reel.

Notes on the song:
The true story of me and my friend Joe Keane. On the day
in question Joe learned the five-part reel, 'Lord Gordon', from
me. He played the tune beautifully on the melodeon. From then
on, every time I play the tune, Joe is in it, alive and laughing.
Nobody would know that, but now you are let in on the secret
with this song.

THE ROSE AND THE HEATHER

(John Hoban)

I've walked these roads for eighty-odd years,
I'm now in the home for the aged.
I've circled The Reek, swam in Dubh Loch,
and I'm none the worse for wear.

My days are now numbered,
my friends pass away,
I'm near the end of life's pathway.
I smile and recall,
those nights in the hall,
between the rose and the heather.

I've lived eighty mixed summers,
carried hay and such work,
it was hard,
but I never regret it.

The fact that I lived on rough, stony ground,
often flooded and clutter'd with nettles.
The music evenings of a long winter's night,
the half-set, song and the story,
kept us alive,
taught us how to survive,
between the rose and the heather.

A man from my village,
once made a fiddle.
The poor crayture just couldn't play it.
My father came home from the fair in Leenane,
where he heard the Raineys play.
He hummed 'The Blackbird',
and 'The Old Copper Plate'.
One day they came from the melodeon.
I was just a boy child,
my thoughts were pure wild,
between the rose and the heather.

Notes on the song:
The first tune I learned, in the Irish traditional music field,
was called 'The Rose in the Heather', a double jig. This song
imagines myself dreaming away at eighty or ninety years of age,
reflecting on a good, decent life, filled with music, song and
dance. Not an easy life mind you, as I try and sing about being
caught between the Devil and the deep-blue sea, between a rock
and a hard place, between the rose, (symbol of love) and the
heather (symbol of childlike pain and brokenness, maybe).

Epilogue

You can sing it.
Qosqo (Cuzco), Peru, March 19, 2009

For the moment, my own music pilgrimage, spanning over five and a half decades, goes on, and is described in stories, songs, poems and pictures. Like the iceberg, or the swan in the water, the main story is hidden under the surface. Here's one of my poems to wrap up the proceedings:

Old Mountain

So now to conclude
and to gather in these verses.
Synthesis, I believe,
in sound, sight and rhythm.
Right now, today,
just singing in the rain,
Peru Rail, on the train
through the Sacred Valley,
high up in the Andes,
en route to Machu Picchu.
It all makes sense to me.
I see the condor, the eagle,
the puma and the snake.
So, Pachamama, mother earth,
old mountain, help us to trust,
to sing, to listen
and finally to walk on
with no fear, nor struggle.

THE LONG FORGOTTEN SAINT

(John Hoban)

I couldn't for the life of me,
remember where we met.
I also had forgotten your name.
Your eyes said more
than a thousand empty words.
Your gentle hands,
have never known shame.

(Chorus)
We talked of birds and trees,
cliffs and raging seas.
We laughed about the times
we'd spend in love.
We watched an artist paint,
a long forgotten saint,
while the music climbs to the mountains to the sky.

The Sunday afternoon you passed away,
I ran to the graveyard to pray.
I lay down a wreath of flowers,
where your head should be.
Then thanked you for setting me free.

Notes on the song:
This is the first song I really wrote. I love the sound of it,
and I love the wee tune in the middle of the song that floated
up the Sruthan river in Castlebar. Sruthan is the Irish word for
an underground stream. It is also the name of the street which
my mother was born on in 1921. It's now called Newantrim
Street.

ON YOUR WAY

(John Hoban)

On your way, dúirt sí liom.
Close your eyes and listen up.
Close your eyes and listen up,
you are loved,
drink from this cup.

Ash to ashes, dúirt sí liom,
shake the dust from off your shoes,
shake the dust from off your shoes,
see each moment, bright and new.

All is well, dúirt sí liom.
From the cradle to the grave,
from the cradle to the grave,
let go and trust, my little brave.

So, ar aghaidh leat, dúirt sí liom.
Don't forget you're not alone,
don't forget you're not alone,
go dté tú slán, on your way home.

Notes on the song:
Said she to me, dúirt sí liom, in a dream, she said a few very
important words to me. "Don't forget you're not alone. Let go
and trust, my little one. Go dté tú slán, may you be kept safe, on
your way home." A song that arrived in a dream. I love this one,
as I love each and every song I sing, and every tune I play.

Every day I live, free at last. Just for today.

Slán agus beannacht.